C000140625

# DEVELOPING OUTCOME ORIENTATED CHILD AND ADOLESCENT MENTAL HEALTH SERVICES

# OO-CAMHS

# A Service Transformation Toolkit

Sami Timimi

Dianne Tetley

Wayne Burgoine

Lincolnshire Partnership **NHS**

NHS Foundation Trust

AuthorHouse™
1663 Liberty Drive
Bloomington, IN 47403
www.authorhouse.com
Phone: 1-800-839-8640

© 2012 Timimi, Tetley and Burgoine. All Rights Reserved.

First published 2012, by Lincolnshire Partnership NHS Foundation Trust

No part of this book may be reproduced, stored in a retrieval system,
or transmitted by any means without the written permission of the author.

Published by AuthorHouse  10/24/2012

ISBN:   978-1-4772-1940-9 (sc)
        978-1-4772-1941-6 (e)

No portion of this publication may be reproduced, copied, or transmitted save with written permission or in accordance
with the provisions of the Copyright, Designs and Patents Act 1988, or under the terms of any licence permitting limited
copying issued by the Copyright Licencing Agency.

The authors have asserted their rights to be identified as the authors of this work in accordance with the Copyright
Designs and Patent Act 1988.

Any people depicted in stock imagery provided by Thinkstock are models,
and such images are being used for illustrative purposes only.
Certain stock imagery © Thinkstock.

This book is printed on acid-free paper.

Because of the dynamic nature of the Internet, any web addresses or links contained in this book may have changed
since publication and may no longer be valid. The views expressed in this work are solely those of the author and do
not necessarily reflect the views of the publisher, and the publisher hereby disclaims any responsibility for them.

Lincolnshire Partnership **NHS**
NHS Foundation Trust

authorHOUSE®

# CONTENTS

# Foreword

Despite the overall effectiveness of youth and family therapy, drop-outs are a substantial problem, many do not benefit, and therapists vary significantly in effectiveness. A relatively new research-proven intervention that involves service users in all decisions that affect their care provides a real solution to these problems. The Partners for Change Outcome Management System or PCOMS (visit www.heartandsoulofchange.com), individualizes services based on client response and preference, prevents drop-outs, and raises the bar of therapists' performance while dramatically improving the results of service users. PCOMS promotes a 'client directed' set of service delivery values: client privilege in determining the benefit of services; an expectation of recovery rather than a focus on illness; an attention to the more 'human' aspects of service delivery in a supportive caring relationship; the instillation of hope; and an appreciation of social justice and the disparate power that exists between the provider and user of services. Routinely requesting, documenting, and responding to client feedback transforms power relations in the immediate therapy and redefines whose voice counts in the broader context of service delivery.

Embracing these values throughout his career, psychiatrist and internationally acclaimed author Sami Timimi, along with research director Dianne Tetley and consultant psychologist Wayne Burgoine, provide a CAMHS and UK friendly interpretation and implementation of PCOMS called Outcome Orientated-Child and Adolescent Mental Health Services or OO-CAMHS. The OO-CAMHS Service Transformation Toolkit provides all you need to get started entering partnerships with your clients to not only improve outcomes but also, as the name suggests, to bring mental health services to a new level. This book does not contain lengthy explanations or academic discussions. Instead, you will find pragmatic steps to get results with your clients while fashioning your work to see clients as human beings whose stories overshadow descriptions of illness, to invite clients to determine their own fate, and to honour the power of partnership in overcoming the struggles of human existence.

Under the leadership of Professor Timimi, OO-CAMHS could very well begin to change the face of mental health care in the UK. With the help of this book, you can be a part of the transformation to involve users as valued stakeholders in the delivery of effective, accountable, and just services.

**Barry Duncan**

February 2012

# Acknowledgements

There are many we would like to thank for their support and encouragement in developing the OO-CAMHS approach and the toolkit. Firstly, the inspiration for our project is Barry Duncan whose passion, devotion and intellect led to him developing a pragmatic way to improve outcomes for those with mental health problems through putting the service user at the centre of mental health services. He has trained us, acted as mentor for our project, and taught us so much about service transformation. For their continued help and enthusiastic support, we want to thank Lincolnshire Partnership NHS Foundation Trust (LPFT) and in particular the Chief Executive Chris Slavin, and the Medical Directors Mostafa Mohanna in the early days of getting OO-CAMHS off the ground and John Brewin since October 2011. However, the views expressed in this toolkit are those of the authors and does not necessarily represent the views of LPFT. For providing intellectual rigour and giving us courage to question assumptions we want to thank members of the Critical Psychiatry Network. For recognising what we had, giving us an innovation award, and helping us develop the project, we want to thank the East Midlands Strategic Health Authority Regional Innovation Fund and in particular the innovation lead, Bernie Stocks. For their permission to reproduce the '© MyOutcomes 2012' quick start users guide we would like to thank Health Factors Empowering Self Care Inc. For their continued hard work, dedication and unending support, we want to thank all staff in LPFT research and effectiveness department and in particular Vicki Dowse for her fantastic administrative support to us. For their work as project facilitators we want to thank James Rathbone and Gill Walker. For their help in developing the audit tool we would like to thank Iram Jalil and Sue Ordish.

We want to reserve a special mention and thanks for the clinicians in the Sleaford and Spalding CAMHS team for their creativity and patience during the days that we struggled to develop this model including Katie Brown, Philomena Cameron, Colin Carman, Marijke De Groot, Samantha Edwards, Karen Hardbattle, and Samuel Ted-Aggrey. Finally we would like to thank the real inspiration behind what the OO-CAMHS project is all about, the moving and heroic young people and families that we have been privileged to meet and work with in CAMHS.

# About the authors

## Sami Timimi

**OO-CAMHS Lead, Certified Trainer and UK Project Leader for Heart and Soul of Change Project**

Sami Timimi is a Consultant Child and Adolescent Psychiatrist and Director of Medical Education at Lincolnshire Partnership NHS Foundation Trust and a Visiting Professor of Child and Adolescent Psychiatry at the University of Lincoln, UK. He writes from a critical psychiatry perspective on topics relating to mental health and has published over a hundred articles and chapters, many in leading peer reviewed journals, on a range of subjects including eating disorders, psychotherapy, behavioural disorders, and cross-cultural psychiatry. He has authored four books, including *Naughty Boys: Anti-Social Behaviour, ADHD and the Role of Culture*, and *A Straight Talking Introduction to Children's Mental Health Problems*. He has co-edited 3 books including *Liberatory Psychiatry: Philosophy, Politics, and Mental Health* with Carl Cohen, and has co-authored with Brian McCabe and Neil Gardner *The Myth of Autism: Medicalising Men's and Boys' Social and Emotional Competence*. Reach Sami at: **stimimi@talk21.com**

## Dianne Tetley

**OO-CAMHS Research Director and Trainer**

Dianne is Assistant Director of Research and Effectiveness at Lincolnshire Partnership NHS Foundation Trust, and an Honorary Research Fellow at the University of Lincoln, UK. Her work is primarily aimed at improving the quality of mental health care for service users. Dianne is an innovator and implementer of quality improvement initiatives. She has received expert training in the set-up and application of client directed outcome informed approaches to clinical work and service delivery. Reach Dianne at: **Dianne_Tetley@hotmail.com**

# Wayne Burgoine

**OO-CAMHS Developer and Trainer**

Wayne is a Senior Clinical Psychologist and Team Manager for the Bairnsdale and Sale CAMHS teams based in the rural and remote regions of Victoria in Australia. As the lead clinician in such a huge geographical area, he is focused on finding innovative ways to support the mental health and well-being of the young people who live across this region. After working for over 6 years in UK CAMHS teams in Lincolnshire, he emigrated to Australia in July 2011, and is now bringing some of the new and innovative ideas that were developed with the UK teams to the other side of the planet. In particular, he is still working with the OO-CAMHS team in Lincolnshire, not only to support the development of the new model in the UK, but also to help to show its applicability to Australian clinical populations too. He welcomes any contact with other clinicians or researchers in Australia who share these interests. Reach Wayne at: **wayneburgoine@hotmail.com**

> **OO-CAMHS is a UK implementation of the Heart and Soul of Change Project's Partners for Change Outcome Management System (PCOMS; Duncan, 2012), a feedback intervention designed to improve the outcomes of mental health services and give patients a voice in all decisions that affect their care.**

OO-CAMHS is a whole service model that incorporates existing evidence on how to improve outcomes, reduce DNAs and dropout rates and save money through improved therapeutic efficiency.[1]

OO-CAMHS is not a model of therapy. It will not remove the inherent 'messiness' of mental health problems and their treatment. Treatments that aim to bring about psychological change belong to the human social relations sphere more than the technical one and like any activity that involves negotiating the interpersonal it is full of nuances and the unexpected. This is part of what the evidence on outcomes confirms. Foregrounding the role of the human encounter in our work is therefore an explicit aim of an OO-CAMHS approach, as is an appreciation that these are more important than which 'technique' is used. OO-CAMHS is a pragmatic and optimistic whole service model. It believes that those with mental health problems can and do recover and this is what services should strive for with everyone it sees. It also believes that unnecessary over-involvement of services can lead to chronic mental health disabilities through focusing on 'disorder', 'disease' and 'dysfunction' in preference to skills and potential resources. This does not mean that the OO-CAMHS model is naïve about the challenges of bringing about positive change. Thus, although not a model of treatment, OO-CAMHS challenges the clinician to use evidence from both research and their patient's feedback to question, challenge, and struggle with thinking through the model of treatment they will use.

The CORE guiding principles of the OO-CAHMS approach are Consultation, Outcome, Relationship, and Ethics of care.

---

[1] We recognize that the term 'patient' is potentially problematic and prefer terms like 'client', 'consumer', and 'service user'. However, we use the term 'patient' throughout this book, as this is the term currently used in the NHS for those whom we see in CAMHS.

# Consultation:

Before embarking on treatment and during treatment think about the external factors/system around the young person. Complex cases can be created by over-intervention that distances people from their existing strengths, abilities and resilience and instead re-enforces feelings of vulnerability and lack of coping.

Aim for not more than one agency working on any one problem at any one time. Use professionals meetings when one agency or more are already involved with the problem/issue the young person has been referred for to clarify which agency will lead on the work. If another agency is leading the work on the presenting problem (for example parent management strategies), consider CAMHS not getting involved until this work is complete. More than one agency working to solve the same problem can result in unnecessary duplication or confusion for the family.

These dynamics can and do occur not only between agencies, but also within them. This means that careful co-ordination should take place if more than one clinician from the Multi-Disciplinary Team is working on treating the problem. As a general rule aim for one clinician at a time, unless there is good reason to have more than one involved at any one time (for example a case that is not making progress and the clinician and family decide to involve another clinician).

# Outcome:

Obtain on-going feedback, session by session, using Patient Related Outcome Measures (PROMs). Make sure the measure is simple and feasible otherwise it will not engage clinicians. OO-CAMHS uses the Outcome Rating Scale (ORS) and Child Outcome Rating Scale (CORS – for 8-12 year olds). These have good psychometric properties and only take a minute or two to complete in follow up appointments (see **'The Outcome and Session Rating Scales'**, pages 26 - 34).

The ORS/CORS should be completed at the start of each session beginning with the first session (whether or not a triage model such as 'Choice And Partnership Approach' (CAPA) is being used). The young person and/or their parents/carers (yp/p/c),[2] depending on who is taking an active part in the treatment, can complete the PROM. **The young person will fill the ORS/CORS about themselves, and the parents/carers will fill in the ORS about their perception of how they believe their child is doing.**

Discuss their ratings to make sure these are properly understood and make an active contribution to shaping the assessment and treatment. Using the ORS/CORS will help quantify yp/p/c's perception of the young person's functioning and progress in treatment.  Use of the ORS/CORS session-by-session can also help the clinician decide whether to focus treatment on the young person, his/her parents, or both.

---

[2] For the sake of brevity we shall refer to the complex of young person and/or their parents/carers as 'yp/p/c' for the rest of this toolkit.

Ask yp/p/c to rate the items in the ORS/CORS in a way that is relevant to the problems that led to the decision to seek treatment because you want the measures to reflect progress in that area.

Low scores identify areas in which the yp/p/c are looking for change, whereas high scores on the different scales can point toward competencies, resources, and social supports. Low scores may also point to areas of risk that may need further exploration.

If the yp/p/c rate above the cut off for clinically significant impairment on the ORS/CORS at the first session, discuss whether they are there because they have been told to come (e.g. by school, GP, social services) but are not particularly motivated to seek treatment, or whether there is a specific issue they wish to address, but overall this is not affecting their day to day functioning. If they are attending because another agency believes they should, but the yp/p/c doesn't, discuss whether consultation with that agency is something that would be helpful. They may also be encouraged to fill the ORS/CORS according to how they imagine the person/agency that wants them to change would do it. If they wish to work on a specific problem, which is within your agency's remit, but overall levels of functioning are good, discuss how you will track progress in addition to session-by-session ORS/CORS (e.g. using one of the scales on the ORS/CORS or an alternative outcome measure such as a goal based outcome measure).

Use the outcome rating scales actively to help shape any intervention. For example, if the ORS/CORS is indicating that family relationships are the biggest area of concern, discuss whether this is what the yp/p/c want to address in the sessions/treatment plan.

Keep a record of the outcome score session-by-session and plot a graph to show progress. Discuss the progress shown on the graph at the beginning of each session with the yp/p/c, to check that it matches their perceptions.

If no improvement has occurred after 5 sessions, discuss with the yp/p/c and/or the Multidisciplinary team. Consider: change of therapeutic approach, change of therapist, agreeing a deadline with the yp/p/c after which a change in approach/therapist/service will be tried if there continues to be no change. *Avoid getting stuck in long-term treatment with no evidence of accompanying improvement.*

If after changes of approach and/or therapist there continues to be no change, discuss with the supervisor and then yp/p/c the possibility that the service is not the right one for them at this time. Consider referral to another service. Remember issues of risk do need to be kept in mind (for example we may not want to discharge actively suicidal patients to no follow up).

Once the yp/p/c are scoring above the cut-off for clinical significance (i.e. are rating that there is no longer clinically significant impairment), or their scores have reached a plateau after a period of improvement, discuss discharge options such as discharging back to the GP, increasing the length of time between appointments, arranging a review appointment several months later and then discharge if all is still going well, or not making another appointment but keeping notes open for a number of months and then discharge if all continues to be well.

# Relationship:

Developing strong therapeutic alliances is key to the OO-CAMHS approach. This means more than just empathy, warmth, and genuineness (important as these are). Meaningful relationships also include agreeing on the models of understanding and goals of the treatment. A capacity to be flexible with how a problem is to be understood and possible solutions discovered is important, particularly when there is a large difference between the cultural beliefs and values of the patient and clinician. Mental health services have a poor track record of engaging those from ethnic minority communities and many from these communities drop out before treatment is completed. Greater openness to models of meaning that are not derived from the dominant culture can assist in improving the chances of meaningful engagement.

Opportunities to develop an alliance start from the first meeting. Models that include a triage with someone other than the person who will continue to offer treatment is therefore a missed opportunity that introduces unnecessary inefficiency for the service and often frustration for the service user. Aim to have the assessment appointment conducted by a clinician who can continue to meet the young person and/or their family should further treatment be offered.

Measure the alliance at the end of each session. Make sure the measure is simple and feasible otherwise it will not engage clinicians. OO-CAMHS uses the Session Rating Scale (SRS) and Child Session Rating Scale (CSRS for 8-12 year olds). These have good psychometric properties and only take a minute or two to complete (see **'The Outcome and Session Rating Scales'**, pages 26 - 34).

From the first session create a culture of strong interest in patient feedback as building strong alliances is important particularly early in treatment. Use the alliance measure as a formal tool to initiate conversations about the alliance and the treatment being offered. Patients are often reluctant to highlight problems or issues they have if simply invited to comment on how they experience the session.

Aim to address and discuss alliance issues before the yp/p/c leave the session. This is often simply to make a plan on how you intend to address any issues raised the next time you meet. Wherever possible avoid leaving alliance issues that have come up, un-discussed.

Talking about the relationship is hard and building a culture of feedback takes a concerted effort. Authentic attention to the alliance via a tool like the SRS helps to build good partnerships.

## Ethics of Care:

Putting patients' strengths, abilities and choices in the centre of the therapeutic process needs clinicians who similarly feel empowered by having their strengths, abilities and therapeutic choices noticed and respected. The OO-CAMHS approach involves building strong relationships with patients, which is mirrored by building strong relationships in the multi-disciplinary team (MDT). Good therapy sees positive value, strengths, acceptance, and abilities in the patients. Good teams see positive value, strengths, acceptance and abilities in the clinicians.

Strong team relationships makes it easier to 'fail successfully' as a clinician, and pass the patient who is not improving in treatment with one member of the team to another clinician in that team.

Just like each patient is different and makes different choices and has a different profile of strengths and challenges, so each clinician is different. Team consultants, managers and supervisors have an important role in noticing and re-enforcing each individual clinician's strengths and helping them develop their therapeutic skills through that clinician's choices.

Building relationships is an on-going process. Make regular opportunities to do things together such as weekly case discussion forums, running groups' together, and regular team development days that can be academic/new service developments/team reflection and so on.

Consult with service users for their ideas on how to improve services.

Use the outcome data in supervision and the overall whole team outcome data in team meetings. This generally provides positive re-enforcement as clinicians and teams can see that they are making a positive difference.

DO NOT strive for a one-size fits all approach for teams. The idea that 'model fidelity' is essential can result in alienating clinicians and leave a team vulnerable to feeling a system is being imposed before clinicians have had an experience of positive change. It can also constrain therapeutic risk taking and creativity. OO-CAMHS teams should expect change to be a constant, as clinicians try new ideas and reflect on the success or otherwise of their work and any initiative.

Use of data needs clarifying with clinicians before adopting OO-CAMHS.

Outcome data should NEVER be used to compare clinicians in a league table of outcomes. Any service that has decided to use data in this manner may develop paranoid dynamics that will hinder the project of improved outcomes for all.

# Introduction

Child and Adolescent Mental Health Services (CAMHS) are underpinned by a philosophy that involves matching the therapeutic intervention to the appropriate diagnosis. However, the international evidence base on factors that most influence outcomes in mental health care finds that matching therapeutic intervention to diagnosis has only a small impact on outcomes when compared to factors such as the strength of the therapeutic relationship.

Furthermore, it is factors outside of therapy (such as availability of social support and socio-economic status) that have the largest impact on outcomes and recovery rates. Decades of outcome research into treatment of psychiatric disorders shows, that despite the development of many new techniques, the outcomes being achieved in studies over 30 years ago are similar to those being achieved now (Smith et al, 1980; Wampold, 2001). Taking this evidence into account when designing and delivering mental health services, means that we have to revisit some of the core assumptions on which services are designed if we are to succeed in making meaningful differences to the chances of the patient's we see improving and recovering.

We are aware that research findings need interpretation and the evidence we outline will inevitably contain our biases in both selection and interpretation. Debates continue and it would be wrong to assume that what we present here represents a final and definitive statement of facts. We therefore encourage readers to do their own critical appraisal of the literature and reach their own conclusions. However, we do believe that we present a reasonable representation of the evidence as it currently stands and have tried in the OO-CAMHS project to translate this evidence into a meaningful clinical approach.

# The Evidence

**This section will cover:**

- An overview of the literature on the factors that influence outcome as a result of treatment for mental health problems.

- An understanding of how the research evidence is relevant to or different from clinical practice.

## Summary of findings

**The variables that influence outcome in order of descending importance is: patient/extra-therapeutic factors, therapeutic alliance, model allegiance, and model of treatment:**

Factors outside of therapy (such as socio-economic status and the availability of social support) have the largest impact on outcomes and recovery rates (Wampold, 2001). Part of this relates to higher dropout rates from treatment for particular groups such as those from a low socio-economic status, with a low level of education, and from an ethnic minority group (Baekeland & Lundwall, 1975; Pekarik, 1992; Edlund et al, 2002).

Within treatment the factor that has the biggest impact on outcomes is the therapeutic alliance (as rated by the patient) with matching treatment model to diagnosis having a small to insignificant impact (Duncan et al, 2010; Wampold, 2001). This relationship between the alliance and outcome seems remarkably robust across treatment modalities and clinical presentations (Castonguay & Beutler, 2005). From those factors within treatment that affect outcome, treatment model has the smallest impact. Between treatment model and therapeutic alliance is model allegiance (Duncan et al, 2010; Wampold, 2001). This refers to the degree to which the therapist believes in the model of treatment they are delivering. Remember these findings are from the research literature and may not apply in the same way to clinical practice. However, one way to think about allegiance in relation to clinical practice is that it may reflect the degree of confidence a clinician has in what they are doing. This in turn can raise a patient's sense of trust in the usefulness of the approach being employed and further raise their sense of hope and expectancy.

It is also worth remembering that many of the 'technologies' (such as specific psychotherapy models) are essentially cultural constructs that have been developed in a particular Western cultural context and researched in predominantly Western societies, raising questions about their suitability when working with communities who don't share similar beliefs and practices. The high dropout rate from mental health treatment for particular groups, such as those from a low socio-economic or ethnic minority background (see above), may reflect a mismatch between systems of meanings employed by the mental health professionals and those more commonly held by these groups.

## The majority of those who receive a mental health treatment will benefit:

Research on the treatment of common psychiatric disorders finds that the average treated person is better off than about 70-80% of the untreated sample (Cooper, 2008; Duncan et al, 2010). In conventional medical research this equates to an effect size change of about 0.8, which is considered a large effect size. This conclusion is based largely on research comparing an active treatment arm to a waiting list control group. As most such studies are relatively short in duration, typically a few months, this mostly refers to the short-term outcomes. Furthermore, many of those who participate in such research are often different to those who frequent mental health services, having undergone careful selection to exclude complexities (such as having more than one psychiatric diagnosis) and having volunteered to take part in the study. As you will see below in the section on differences between outcomes found in research and those found in practice, these large effect sizes are not always apparent in studies of clinical practice, particularly in CAMHS. None the less it is important to note that research confirms the effectiveness of common treatments for mental health problems and therefore supports the importance and impact that mental health services such as CAMHS can have on people's lives.

## Treatment largely works through the mediation of 'common factors' shared by different theoretical approaches:

The belief that one (or more) therapy would prove superior to others for particular conditions has found little support. This was becoming increasingly evident by the late eighties/early nineties (Norcross & Goldfried, 1992). Besides an occasional significant finding for a particular therapy, the critical mass of data and its meta-analysis has revealed little in the way of clinically significant differences in effectiveness between the various 'bona fide' treatment models for psychological distress (Wampold, 2001). Despite the development of many new techniques, the outcomes being achieved in studies conducted over 30 years ago have remained broadly similar to those being achieved now (Smith et al, 1980; Wampold, 2001). Furthermore, even within treatment models, there is little evidence to support that any components of a model considered crucial is in fact so. Several studies have shown that most of the specific features of CBT can be dispensed with without adversely affecting outcomes (Jacobson et al, 1996; Longmore & Worrell, 2007). This is also true for other therapies. Ahm & Wampold's (2001) meta-analysis of 27 component studies concluded that the effect size for the difference between a package with or without components considered critical was not significantly different from zero.

As far back as the 1930s Saul Rosenzweig (1936) concluded that, since no form of psychotherapy or healing was without cures to its credit, its success is not reliable proof of the validity of its theory. Instead, he suggested that some implicit 'common factors' maybe more important than the particular techniques employed. Rosenzweig's insight turned out to be more empirically supportable than the specific techniques of each model (Duncan et al, 2010). Wampold concludes from his meticulous review of the literature, that, "*Decades of psychotherapy research have failed to find a scintilla of evidence that any specific ingredient is necessary for therapeutic change*" (Wampold, 2001, p204).

Top in terms of impact on outcome are factors outside of therapy such as relative poverty, degree of motivation and social support. From within therapy the alliance as perceived by the patient is the most robust predictor of outcome. Orlinsky et al, (2004) observe, "*the quality of the patient's participation… [emerges] as the most important determinant in outcome*" (p. 324). Patients who are more engaged and involved in therapeutic processes are likely to receive greater benefit from therapy. The alliance is of course a two way process involving therapists capacity to engage with patients in meaningful ways, as well as the capacity and motivation of patients for engaging in therapy. Much of the literature suggests that patients' who are ready and willing to make changes are more likely to develop a positive therapeutic alliance and thus do better in treatment (Cooper, 2008).

This common factors perspective seems to hold in marriage and family approaches (Shadish & Baldwin, 2002), and child and adolescent therapies (Spielmans et al., 2007; Miller et al., 2008).

As with adults, extra-therapeutic factors have the biggest impact on outcomes for treatments with children and young people. For example, few studies find that a diagnosis of ADHD is independently associated with continuing impairments, whereas most studies on outcomes for those with a diagnosis of ADHD find that co-morbidity with conduct disorder, together with adverse environmental conditions (such as socio-economic disadvantage, maternal depression, and marital discord), rather than ADHD severity per se are associated with the most adverse outcomes (Barkley et al, 2004; Biederman et al, 1996; Fergusson et al, 2007; Lee & Hinshaw, 2004). A diagnosis of ADHD is thus by itself not a good predictor of future outcomes, but extra-therapeutic factors are.

Karver and colleagues (2005) concluded that the success of 'empirically supported' treatments is likely to depend on the presence of common process factors in youth and family therapy. In a meta-analysis of treatments for depression in children, Weisz et al, (2006) found that, although various treatments were more effective than no treatment, no difference in outcome was found between cognitive and non-cognitive approaches. Spielmans et al (2007) in a meta-analysis of component studies found that the theoretically purported critical ingredients of CBT are not specifically ameliorative for child and adolescent depression and anxiety as full CBT treatments offered no significant benefit over treatments with only components of the full model. These are just a few examples of a robust database that concludes that, overall, common factors are more important determinants of outcome than the specific ingredients of a therapeutic model.

## Matching treatment model to diagnosis has a small and largely insignificant impact on outcomes:

In the treatment of common adult mental health conditions, few meaningful differences in outcomes are found between competing approaches intended to be therapeutic for a particular presentation, providing treatment conditions are equal and the issue of the therapeutic allegiance of the researchers is controlled for (Anderson et al, 2010; Benish et al., 2008; Imel & Wampold, 2008; Wampold, 2007). Thus, no clinically significant differences in outcome have been found between different treatment approaches in general (Wampold, 2001), in depression (Wampold et al., 2002), in PTSD (Benish et al, 2008), and in alcohol use disorders (Imel et al., 2008). This is also evident in 'real life' clinical encounters not just research projects. For example, in a review of over 5000 cases treated in a variety of National Health Service settings in the UK, only a very small proportion of the variance in outcome could be attributed to psychotherapeutic technique, as opposed to non-specific effects such as the therapeutic relationship (Stiles et al, 2008). This lack of specificity is also found for child and adolescent disorders.

As with the adult outcome literature, within treatment there is little evidence to support that matching a treatment model to a diagnosis differentiates which treatment is more likely to work and which is not. Miller et al (2008) conducted a meta-analysis to determine whether differences in efficacy exist among treatment approaches in therapies for youth. Included were all studies published between 1980 and 2005 involving participants 18 years of age or younger with diagnoses of depression, anxiety, conduct disorder, or attention-deficit/hyperactivity disorder that contained direct comparisons among two or more treatment methods intended to be therapeutic. They found that once researcher allegiance was controlled for, evidence of any differences among the treatments disappeared.

## High rates of treatment drop out are evident in most mental health services:

Treatment drop out is a significant problem in the delivery of mental health care averaging nearly 50% for many services (Wierzbicki & Pekarik, 1993). Hansen et al, (2002), using a national data base of over 6000 patients in the US, reported a sobering picture of routine clinical care in which only 20% of patients improved as compared to the 57-67% rates typical of RCTs, with much of the problem being related to early treatment drop out.

For children and adolescents, the range for dropout rates varies from 28% to 85% (Garcia & Weisz, 2002; Kazdin, 1996, 2004). For example, Kazdin (2004) reports that 40–60% of youth who begin treatment drop out against advice.

Thus, despite the fact that the general efficacy for treatment of mental health problems is good in research settings, not everyone benefits, with one of the big problems confronting the field being the high rate of patients who drop out from treatment.

## Clinicians are poor at understanding their efficacy and predicting those who will drop out of or not benefit from treatment:

Not surprisingly, although rarely discussed, some therapists are much better at securing positive results than others. Therapist effectiveness varies, but clinicians are not very good at judging their own. Clinical decision-making it seems relies on the clinician's personal judgement and experience and they often continue to be confident in their decision making whatever the outcome. For example, a study by Sapyta et al, (2005) asked 143 clinicians to rate their performance in comparison to other clinicians from A+ to F. Two-thirds considered themselves A or better; 90% considered themselves in the top 25%, and not one therapist rated him or herself as below average. Another study found that therapists on average rated their overall clinical skills and effectiveness at the 80th percentile (a statistical impossibility), less than 4% considered themselves average, and not a single person in the study rated his or her performance below average (Walfish et al, 2010). Moreover, clinicians routinely fail to identify patients who are not progressing or deteriorating and at most risk of dropout and negative outcome (Hannan et al., 2005). The majority of therapists have never measured their outcomes and do not know how effective they are (Hansen et al., 2002). The consistent overestimating of personal effectiveness and lack of feedback on their 'performance' as therapists can put patients at risk for higher rates of dropout and negative outcomes.

## The clinical population has some different characteristics from the research population and less evidence of significant change as a result of treatment:

Much of the research data comes from patients and families who have volunteered for research, and study inclusion criteria often means more complex multi-problem presentations have been excluded. The typical clinic population has many who have multi-problem presentations and some who feel ambivalent about engaging with services.

Thus although some studies have found that outcomes following treatment in clinical settings are comparable to those found in research (e.g. Stiles et al, 2008), others have not. For example, Hansen et al (2002), using a national database of over 6000 patients in the US, reported a picture of routine clinical care in which only 20% of patients improved.

There are number of reasons why patients in clinical practice don't do as well as those in research including; exclusion criteria for research tends to keep out patients who are more difficult to treat (for example those with co-morbidity), and variability among therapists is the rule rather than the exception.

In child and adolescent mental health some evidence suggests even larger differences in outcome between research and clinical practice, than for adults. Thus, although the effect size for outcomes in controlled studies is large, some studies have found that for traditional treatment in community CAMH services, the effect size is close to zero (Weisz et al, 1995, 1999, 2000).

Other evidence finds that changes to service configuration including allocating extra resources has little impact on outcomes. The Fort Bragg evaluation described the implementation, quality, costs, and outcomes of a $94 million demonstration project designed to improve mental health outcomes for children and adolescents who were referred for mental health treatment. Extensive mental health data were collected on children and their families and evaluations continued for several years.  Outcomes in the experimental service were no better than those in the treatment as usual group, despite the considerable extra costs incurred (Bickman et al, 1995; 2000). This finding was then replicated in the Stark County evaluation study that examined a new system of care designed to provide comprehensive mental health services to children and adolescents. Again there were no differences in outcomes when compared with care received outside the new system, despite the extra costs (Bickman et al, 1997).

## Those who benefit from treatment usually show evidence of positive change from early sessions:

The longer patients attend therapy without experiencing a positive change, the greater the likelihood they will experience a negative or null outcome or drop out from treatment (Duncan, et al, 2010). Howard, et al, (1986) found that approximately 30% of patients improve by the second session, 70% to 75% by six months and 85% by one year. Although the rate of patient change differs somewhat from person to person, early response in therapy is a strong indicator of eventual outcome, making the monitoring of improvement from the start of therapy important.

## Focusing on patient resources rather than problems may improve outcomes:

In a number of studies examining the content of therapeutic sessions, Gassman & Grawe (2006) found that problem focussed and resource focussed conversations play different roles in the process of change, with problem activation alone less likely to lead to therapeutic progress. Successful therapists chose different degrees of and different timing in applying the two (problem focussed and resource activation conversations) than unsuccessful ones and made better use of patients' existing resources. This supports a previous observation that patients who attribute change through treatment to their own efforts and resources rather than an external agent (such as a medication) are more likely to maintain therapeutic gains (Frank, 1976; Lieberman, 1978).

## Using routine and on-going feedback can improve outcome, reduce non-attendance, and reduce the number of patients 'stuck' in treatment with no improvement:

Howard et al, (1996) were the first to advocate for the systematic evaluation of patient response to treatment during the course of therapy, but it was feedback pioneer Michael Lambert who brought this idea to fruition. Using the Outcome Questionnaire 45, Lambert has conducted five randomised controlled trials and all five have demonstrated significant gains for formal feedback (on progress in treatment) groups over treatment as usual (TAU) for patients rated as being 'at-risk for a negative outcome'. From those deemed at risk of a poor outcome, 22% of TAU cases reached reliable improvement and clinically significant change compared with 33% for feedback to therapist groups, 39% for feedback to therapists and patients, and 45% when feedback was supplemented with support tools such as measures of the alliance (Lambert, 2010). The addition of empirical feedback on progress in treatment, without new techniques or models of treatment and leaving therapists to practice as they saw fit, enabled two times the amount of patients at-risk of not improving from treatment to benefit. A recent meta-analysis of these studies (Lambert & Shimokawa, 2011) found that those in feedback groups had 3.5 higher odds of experiencing reliable change and less than half the odds of experiencing deterioration.

Lambert's pioneering work has led to a growing interest in the merits of using feedback measures to highlight problems such as little or no clinical improvement or a poor therapeutic alliance and adjust treatments accordingly. The challenge as always has been how to turn findings and processes used in a research context into one feasible for the realities of busy clinical practice. Poor clinician uptake of any approach is usually a rate-limiting factor for the uptake of any new idea. A number of groups have been attempting to make this leap from research into clinical practice, with the best-known and most successful example being the Partners for Change Outcome Management System (PCOMS) (Duncan, 2012).

PCOMS is a project developed in America and devoted to empirically-derived clinical practices, through incorporating predictors of therapeutic success into an outcome management system that includes simple, easy to use ratings of both therapeutic progress and alliance (Duncan & Sparks, 2010). PCOMS uses two brief scales, the Outcome Rating Scale (ORS) and the Session Rating Scale (SRS) to measure the patient's perspective of benefit and the alliance, respectively. The development of PCOMS has included research and publications in peer reviewed journals to establish psychometric validation of its instruments (Bringhurst et al, 2006; Campbell & Hemsley, 2009; Duncan et al, 2003; Gillaspy & Murphy, 2011; Miller et al, 2003; Miller et al, 2006). The ORS and SRS exhibit good internal consistency and test-retest reliability despite the ultra-brief nature (four items) of these measures. PCOMS has been shown in a number of randomized clinical trials to significantly improve effectiveness in clinical settings (Anker et al, 2009; Anker et al, 2010; Reese et al, 2009; Reese et al, 2010).

The Outcome Rating Scale (ORS) and the Session Rating Scale (SRS) are both four-item measures designed to track outcome and the therapeutic alliance, respectively. They were based on Lambert's continuous assessment model and the associated questionnaires he developed. In RCTs of PCOMs, use of the ORS/SRS (as part of PCOMS) resulted in improved treatment outcomes when compared to treatment as usual (TAU) (Anker et al, 2009; Anker et al, 2010; Reese et al, 2009; Reese et al, 2010). Although three of the studies focused on individual therapy, Anker et al, (2009) and Reese et al, (2010) extended evaluation of PCOMS to couples therapy. Patients in PCOMS achieved reliable change in significantly fewer sessions than TAU.

Several services that have adopted PCOMS as a whole service model have reported substantial changes in terms of big reductions in the number of patients who remain in long-term treatment, in DNA rates, and in complaints. The improved therapeutic efficiency of these services has also led to significant cost savings too (Duncan & Sparks, 2010). It is because PCOMS has established an empirical record of improving outcomes in both research and clinical settings, OO-CAMHS based its own model on this project.

## Predictors of success from treatment include: level of distress at start of treatment, patient's rating of alliance, and evidence of early change in treatment:

The following factors have been shown to be good predictors of eventual outcome from treatment: level of distress (higlevels at the start predicts greater improvement), duration of therapy without positive change, early change in treatment, patients' rating of the alliance and their degree of engagement with treatment (Cooper, 2008).

The longer patients attend treatment without evidence of a positive change, the greater the likelihood they will experience a poor outcome or drop out of treatment (Duncan et al, 2010). Although the rate of change differs somewhat from person to person, early response in treatment is a good indicator of eventual outcome, making the monitoring of progress from the start of treatment important (Howard et al, 1986).

Patients' rating of the alliance is a consistent and reliable predictor of treatment outcome (Duncan et al, 2010), with Orlinsky, et al (2004) observing that the "*the quality of the patient's participation… [emerges] as the most important determinant in outcome*" (p. 324). Patients who are more engaged and involved in therapeutic processes are likely to receive greater benefit from treatment, with the best predictor of engagement being the alliance according to the patient.

There is also some evidence to suggest improvement in the alliance over the course of treatment results in better outcomes than alliances, which start and stay good or deteriorate over time (Anker et al, 2009; Anker et al., 2010).

## Weak or non-predictors of good outcomes: matching treatment model to diagnosis, profession, years of experience, and model fidelity in treatment delivery:

A number of studies have identified variables that have little or no correlation with the outcome of treatment. These include: patient gender, diagnosis, and previous treatment history (Wampold & Brown, 2005) and clinician gender, years of experience, professional discipline, theoretical orientation, amount of supervision, personal therapy, and use of evidence-based practices (Beutler et al., 2004; Hubble et al., 2010; Nyman et al, 2010; Miller et al, 2007; Wampold & Brown, 2005). In practice terms there is little evidence to support the importance of the model/ technique of therapy used (Benish, et al, 2008; Imel et al., 2008; Miller et al, 2008; Wampold et al., 1997; Wampold et al., 2002), matching model of treatment to diagnosis (Wampold, 2001), and adherence/fidelity to a particular treatment approach (Duncan & Miller, 2005; Webb et al, 2010).

## Psychotropic medication may be beneficial in improving short-term outcomes, but does not appear to improve long-term outcomes (when compared to psychological approaches) and may be associated with greater risk of adverse events, relapse, and developing chronic symptoms than psychological approaches:

The same principles of non-specific factors being more important than matching a drug to a diagnosis, can be found operating when using psychoactive drug treatments. Thus it is now recognised that instead of correcting imbalances, the evidence supports the view that pharmacological agents may be conceptualised as inducing particular psychological states which, though not specifically related to diagnosis, is nonetheless the basis for their usefulness (Moncrieff, 2009). In clinical practice the few categories of psychoactive medications used in psychiatry (the SSRIs, major tranquilisers, benzodiazepines, Lithium, and anti-epileptics) are often used in a non-diagnosis specific way. For example, SSRIs are claimed to be efficacious in conditions as disparate as borderline personality disorder, depression, obsessive compulsive disorder, anorexia nervosa, bulimia, panic disorder, generalised anxiety disorder, social phobias, and so forth. As a psychoactive substance SSRIs would appear to do 'something' to the mental state, but that something is not diagnosis specific. Like alcohol, which will produce inebriation in a person with schizophrenia, obsessive compulsive disorder, depression, or someone with no psychiatric diagnosis; SSRIs will also impact individuals in ways that are not specific to diagnosis.

Similarly, major tranquilisers (misnamed anti-psychotics) have also been advocated for the treatment of depression, anxiety disorders, bipolar affective disorder, personality disorders, ADHD, as well as schizophrenia, a list that contains considerable overlap with that found for SSRIs.

Psychiatric drug treatments, like psychological treatments, rely more on non-specific factors than disease-specific therapeutic effects. For example, it is generally assumed that drugs marketed as 'antidepressants' work through their pharmacological effects on specific neurotransmitters in the CNS, reversing particular states of 'chemical imbalance'. However, not only is there little evidence to support the theory that depressed people have a 'chemical imbalance', but, in addition, the evidence points to placebo effects being more important than any neuro-pharmacological ones. Thus several meta-analyses have concluded that most of the benefits from 'antidepressants' can be explained by the placebo effect, with only a small amount of the variance (about 20%) attributable to the drug – a small amount moreover that is unlikely to be clinically significant for the vast majority of patients (Kirsch et al, 2008). Even this small advantage that antidepressants appear to have over placebo is likely to be attributable to 'un-blinding' of patients through patients recognising, by the presence of side effects, that they are on the active drug (Kirsch, 2009). In the short-term therefore there is little evidence to support that using an anti-depressant improves recovery rates compared to placebo. More importantly, long-term outcome studies find that those who recover through medication have higher relapse rates when compared to those who recover through psychotherapy (Kirsch, 2009), casting doubt as to whether SSRIs should have any place in the treatment of depression.

Studies investigating the degree to which non-technical factors, such as the therapeutic relationship, affect outcome, have found that even with psychoactive drug treatments these factors are more influential than the drug alone. Thus having a good relationship with the prescribing doctor is a stronger predictor of a positive response to an anti-depressant than just taking the drug regardless of who prescribes it (Wampold & Brown, 2006; Sparks et al, 2008).

The lack of treatment specificity is not limited to the more common and less severe presentations. Thus, although drugs marketed as 'antipsychotic' are often claimed to reverse a biochemical imbalance in psychotic patients, no such imbalance has been demonstrated. Furthermore, researchers have long been aware of a perplexing finding in cross-cultural studies. Research, including that carried out by the World

Health Organisation, over the course of 30 years and starting in the early 1970s, shows that patients outside North America and Europe have significantly lower relapse rates and are significantly more likely to have made a 'full' recovery and show lower degrees of impairment when followed up over several years despite most having limited or no access to 'anti-psychotic' medication. It seems that the regions of the world with the most resources to devote to mental illness – the best technology, medicines, and the best-financed academic and private-research institutions – had the most troubled and socially marginalised patients (Hopper et al, 2007). Once again the impact of our technologies seem to be minimal compared to common factors, in this case most likely to be the effects of 'extra-therapeutic' factors such as family support, community cohesion and a greater tolerance for behaviours and experiences considered a sign of 'illness' and 'dangerousness' in the West.

Studies on treatments involving medication for children or adolescents make similar findings. For example the Treatment of Adolescent Depression Study (TADS), which is the largest trial ever conducted for childhood depression, claimed to show an advantage for fluoxetine, especially when combined with cognitive–behavioural therapy (CBT) (Treatment of Adolescent Depression Study Team, 2004). However, there were flaws in the way they reported their data. TADS consisted of two separate randomised studies: a double-blind comparison of fluoxetine and placebo and an unmasked comparison between CBT alone and fluoxetine plus CBT. The lack of participant masking and placebo control in the latter group is likely to exaggerate the benefit seen in the fluoxetine plus CBT group, who received more face-to-face contact and knew (as did their doctors) that they were not receiving placebo. Comparing results across all four groups is therefore misleading. The only valid finding from the TAD study is the lack of a statistical advantage of fluoxetine over placebo on the primary measure, the Children's Depression Rating Scale. A 'common factors' perspective would then predict that once participants are free from allegiance effects (which clearly favoured medication) any group differences would disappear. A follow up study indeed found that the outcomes for all groups converged by week 30 (March et al, 2007). A similar process happened in the largest study of treatment for children with ADHD, the Multimodal Treatment Study of ADHD (MTA) (MTA Co-operative Group, 1999). At 14 months the authors concluded that medication was superior to behaviour therapy, a finding most likely to reflect author bias in study design and interpretation. However, by 3-years all the advantages for those on medication had been lost, although those exposed to medication experienced more adverse effects (Timimi, 2008).

Thus the common factors perspective holds for children and young people including those who are prescribed medication. As children and young people's nervous system is still developing, then from a 'first do no harm' perspective, we believe the evidence supports taking a position of making psychosocial treatments the first line for all mental health problems in young people. Use of psychotropic medication should then be limited to those with more severe impairments and used in a pragmatic, non-diagnostic specific manner, for as short a time as possible and at as low a dose as possible (Timimi, 2009).

# The OO-CAMHS Project

**This section will cover:**

- The reasons for developing the OO-CAMHS model.

- UK projects that include whole service models for CAMHS and/or outcome measure development, namely:

  - CAMHS Outcomes Research Consortium (CORC),

  - Choice And Partnership Approach (CAPA),

  - The Children and Young People's Improving Access to Psychological Therapies (CYP-IAPT).

- The Partners for Change Outcome Management System (PCOMS) – an American project that is the inspiration for developing the OO-CAMHS model.

The OO-CAMHS project aims to build a whole model service model that incorporates key aspects of the evidence cited above. OO-CAMHS is a UK implementation of the Heart and Soul of Change Project's, Partners for Change Outcomes Management Systems (PCOMS) adapted to a UK and CAMHS context.

A number of 'drivers' spurred us on to developing this model. These include: growing familiarity with the outcome literature, a desire to develop a whole service model to improve outcomes that incorporates the evidence base in a clinically meaningful way, the widespread use by UK CAMHS services of the CAMHS Outcome Research Consortium (CORC) for outcome measurement, and the widespread use of Choice and Partnership Approach (CAPA) by UK CAMHS services for whole service organisation and process. It was our opinion, an opinion that seemed to be shared by most colleagues we spoke to whose CAMHS service had adopted these latter two projects, that neither project on their own had either the evidential basis or all the elements needed to do what we wanted to do, and that is be part of a service that operated a model that maximised the chances of the service improving outcomes for the young people we see at the same time as minimising the likelihood of adverse outcomes. This does not mean that those two projects are without value and we share similar objectives and some similar methodologies; just that on their own they are insufficient for addressing the sort of service transformation that we were aiming at.

Since we developed the OO-CAMHS model a new national project has got underway, the Children and Young People's Improving Access to Psychological Therapies (CYP-IAPT) project. We see potential for genuine partnerships with each of these 3 projects (CORC, CAPA, and CYP-IAPT) and hope that we can all learn from each other about what helps build CAMHS services that improve the lives of as many young people as possible.

## CORC

The CAMHS Outcomes Research Consortium (CORC) is a collaboration between child and adolescent mental health services across the UK with the aim of instituting a common model of routine outcome evaluation and analysing the data derived. (Further details about the CORC project can be found at **http://www.corc.uk.net**)

*CORC's mission statement*: CORC aims to foster the effective and routine use of outcome measures in work with children and young people (and their families and carers) who experience mental health and emotional wellbeing difficulties. It aims to do this through collaboration with its members, academic consultants, and learning partners, sharing ideas and good practice in order to:–

- Develop usable and effective models of routine outcome measurement.

- Promote and encourage the use of routine outcome measurement as an integrated part of any organisation working with child mental health and emotional wellbeing.

- Develop ways to meaningfully interpret the outcomes data.

- Use outcomes data to encourage learning and improve practice in work with the individual child, young person, their family and carers; as well as to encourage learning and improve practice at the level of: practitioner, team, organisation, and policy.

CORC started as a collaboration between five services in 2002 and, following support from the National CAMHS Support Service (NCSS) and facilitation from the National Institute of Mental Health England (NIMHE), opened to wider membership in April 2004.

CORC primarily recommends use of the Strengths and Difficulties Questionnaire (SDQ), the CHI (child) Experience of Service Questionnaire (CHI-ESQ), and the Children's Global Assessment Scale (CGAS). The Goal Based Outcome measure (GBO) was also approved a couple of years ago and in the last year other measures approved for use by CORC include the Outcome Rating Scale (ORS) and Session Rating Scale (SRS), which are the measures we recommend.

SDQ is a symptom and functioning based measure of the child's behaviour and the impact this is having on different areas of the child's life, to be completed by parents and relevant children seen by the service at assessment and between 4-8 months after initial contact (For more information on this measure, go to **http://www.sdqinfo. com**). The ESQ is a measure of service satisfaction. Parents and relevant children seen by the service, as long as they have attended at least one session, complete it. The CGAS is a practitioner-rated global measure of functioning for children and young people. It is completed for all children seen by the service after assessment and 6-months after initial contact. Goal Based Outcomes (GBOs) compare how far a young person feels they have moved towards reaching a goal they set at the beginning of an intervention using a simple scale from 0-10 to capture the change.

The main issue with CORC measures is that return rates for second scores on the main patient related comparative measure, the SDQ, are low. For many years it has run at 10-25% or lower, thus no reliable and therefore valid outcome data has been produced by this methodology. It seems young people and their families are just not filling in and returning the second ratings. Thus the CORC project has failed for many years to reach its stated aims and became unpopular with many clinicians, as they were unable to see the outcome measures relevance to their clinical practice.

CORC are trying to address these shortcomings by widening the range of approved measures in order to support more locally based projects (such as OO-CAMHS) and has moved toward investigating and supporting the use of session-by-session outcome measures. However, the session by session measures that CORC have developed, remain wedded to a 'symptom/diagnostic' cluster approach, which we see as potentially problematic, and currently there is no data available on their proposed session-by-session measures from a research, clinical practice, or service transformation perspective.

The OO-CAMHS project has received support and acknowledgement from CORC, and we are committed to working with CORC to help contribute toward achieving their and our goals.

# CAPA

*Choice And Partnership Approach (CAPA)* "*is a systemic approach to service organisation and to the relationship with the user / patient. It aims to put the user at the centre. To aid their choices we should use our expertise. To be the most effective we need to smooth our processes and make every step add value. We must deliver our resources by planning as a whole system and layering skills whenever possible.*" (**http://www.capa.co.uk**)

CAPA introduced some useful ideas for clinical practice, though these are more 'common sense' than evidence based (such as giving patients choices at the assessment, every step adding value, and layering skills). Its main contribution however is as an organisational aid to developing administrative systems (such as diary slots for teams to do 'choice' appointments, calculating service capacity, and working out how many 'choice' and how many 'partnership' appointments each clinician should aim to have). These are important and valuable developments and CAPA has helped many services transform their administrative and overall service processes resulting in reduced waiting lists, improved capacity, and improved team morale. We are very supportive of the CAPA team's efforts and ideas and believe they have positively influenced CAMHS whole team organisation in teams across the world.

Its main weakness is the separation of 'assessment' (choice) appointments from 'treatment' (partnership) appointments, often with different clinicians providing the choice and then partnership appointments. As patients' form alliances from the first meeting and good alliances are crucial to good outcomes, such a separation means that an unnecessary extra step is introduced into the process for those who decide to carry on to the 'partnership' stage. Many patients will have to start the process of forming a therapeutic relationship all over again, increasing the inefficiency of the process, not to mention the inconvenience for the family. In the OO-CAMHS model we believe that trying to match the clinician with the patient from the first appointment is desirable and the general expectation is that the clinician will continue working with the family if it is agreed that further input is desired. Other aspects of CAPA such as 'care bundles' (grouping together several interventions that are offered to the family simultaneously) are not in our view based on the best evidence with regards outcome and can cause unnecessary duplication, and confusion. This does not mean we are against more than one clinician working with a case at any one time, but do think decisions on involving another clinician or treatment, should be linked to outcome and tested for its efficacy by collecting outcome data to inform decisions about multi-professional interventions.

However, these potentially problematic aspects of CAPA are all 'adjustable' in our view and compatibility of CAPA with OO-CAMHS is easy to achieve by being mindful of the issues raised above. The OO-CAMHS project developed within the context of a CAMHS team using a CAPA model that was adapted in the manner described in this toolkit. For example we still run choice clinics in the CAPA format, but try to think ahead of who may be best to carry out the choice to reduce the chances of needing to change clinician if the choice leads to partnership appointments. As CAPA shares the same core values as OO-CAMHS, we believe the two models are comfortably compatible with each other.

## CYP-IAPT

*The Children and Young People's Improving Access to Psychological Therapies (CYP-IAPT)* is a programme is funded by the UK government's department of health and aims build on the learning from the adult IAPT programme. It acknowledges that the needs of children and young people and the systems that support and surround them are different to those of adults, and so, although it shares certain key features and principles, it also has some differences to the adult IAPT programme. CYP- IAPT focuses on improving the skills of the existing CAMHS workforce and has decided to achieve this by training staff in the manualised implementation of Cognitive Behaviour Therapy packages or Parenting programmes (with other approaches being included later in the roll out). Training in these approaches for staff at phase one sites began in September 2011. Implementation post training will (as in the adult IAPT) require staff to use session-by-session outcome rating scales, though these will be based on 'symptom cluster' type rating scales (see http://www.iapt.nhs.uk/cyp-iapt/).

The CYP-IAPT is a costly scheme. It involves providing training for already trained staff despite the lack of evidence that such training improves outcomes and contributes to service transformation. If the experience of adult IAPT, that has been running for several years, is replicated, then we can expect an expensive service with no accompanying improvement in outcomes overall. According to reports compiled by the Artemis Trust (Evans, 2011 a and b), the average number of patients achieving recovery for a fixed expenditure of £100,000 treated by an IAPT service appears to be lower (49) than for pre-IAPT primary care counselling services (115) or voluntary sector counselling services (78). In addition recovery rates, as a percentage of patients referred, seems to be lower for IAPT services than comparable services (Pre-IAPT primary care psychological therapy services, university counselling services, and Employee Assistance Program counselling services). If these findings are confirmed as representative, then it is a truly remarkable achievement that the government have spent large amounts of taxpayers' money creating an expensive service that has poorer outcomes than cheaper alternatives that were already in existence before IAPT. The expectation was that IAPT would improve outcomes as it uses National Institute of Clinical Excellence (NICE) guidelines and session by session by session ratings of outcome.

The experience of IAPT reminds us that improving services is not just down to using session-by-session rating scales, which, as if by magic, will change everything. In IAPT, session-by-session ratings are used as a 'add on' to the medical model manner of matching treatment to diagnosis. As Bickman et al, (1995; 1997; 2000) found in their evaluation of the Fort Bragg and Stark County projects (see page 12) more expensive services don't necessarily lead to better outcomes.

However, in addition to training staff in CBT or parenting, CYP-IAPT also involves a more ambitious and potentially more interesting 'service transformation' objective, hoping to influence the whole CAMHS team (not just those who get trained in the specific therapies) to use more feedback and think more carefully and critically about their work. Thus there is an opportunity to expand services and access to psychological therapies for young people in a positive way as the national CYP-IAPT group starts to explore what may be needed to develop genuine service transformations that can improve outcomes, efficiency and the influence of the service user's voice and choices. Early indications give ground for encouragement, that CYP-IAPT is engaging in a positive, thoughtful and collaborative manner in this aspect of their objectives.

## PCOMS

*Partners for Change Outcome Management System (PCOMS)* is a project developed in America and devoted to empirically-derived clinical practices, through incorporating predictors of therapeutic success into an outcome management system that includes simple, easy to use ratings of both therapeutic progress and alliance (Duncan, 2012; Duncan & Sparks, 2010) (see **www.heartandsoulofchange.com**). PCOMS uses two brief scales, the Outcome Rating Scale (ORS) and the Session Rating Scale (SRS) to measure the patient's perspective of benefit and the alliance, respectively (see **'The Outcome and Session Rating Scales'**, pages 26 - 34). PCOMS has been shown in a number of randomized clinical trials (RCTs) to significantly improve effectiveness in clinical settings (Anker et al, 2009; Anker et al, 2010; Reese et al, 2009; Reese et al, 2010).

In RCTs of PCOMs, use of the ORS/SRS (as part of PCOMS) resulted in improved treatment outcomes when compared to treatment as usual (TAU) (Miller et al, 2006; Anker et al, 2009; Anker et al, 2010; Reese et al, 2009; Reese et al, 2010). Although three of the studies focused on individual therapy, Anker et al, (2009) and Reese, et al, (2010) extended evaluation of PCOMS to couples therapy. Patients in PCOMS achieved reliable change in significantly fewer sessions than TAU.

PCOMS has demonstrated the potential to improve outcomes and therapeutic efficiency in real services not just in research projects. The following are examples of real life services that have adopted PCOMS as a whole service model (see Duncan and Sparks, 2010):

**Community Health and Counselling Services in Maine** provides community-based mental health services to adults and children. Over 750 clinical staff work in the organisation. The following is comparison data following adoption of PCOMS: reduced number of patients seen for more than one year from 655 (pre-PCOMS) to 321 (post-PCOMS); reduced number patients seen more than two years, from 227 (pre-PCOMS) to 94 (post-PCOMS); number of 'No Shows' reduced by 30%.

**Southwest Behavioral Health Services in Arizona** provides comprehensive mental health services and has over 400 clinical staff. Two years following the adoption of PCOMS they had achieved:  decrease in the average length of an episode of care in children's' services from 315 days to 188; adult services length of stay decreased from an average 322 days to 158; 'no shows' decreased by 47%.

**Center for Family Service of Palm Beach County, Florida** provides counselling, and related services and has over 100 clinical staff. Three years following implementation of PCOMS they had achieved: reduced 'drop outs' by 50% and 'no shows' by 25%; using 40% fewer sessions to achieve program goals; use of fewer resources without sacrificing patient satisfaction; a decreased by 80% in the number of long term therapy cases where no benefit was being achieved; and a decreased in the number and frequency of patient grievances and complaints to almost zero.

# OO-CAMHS

*OO-CAMHS is a UK implementation of the Heart and Soul of Change Project's Partners for Change Outcome Management Systems.* Adapting the evidence from the outcome literature and the successful PCOMS model to working with children and adolescents means facing particular challenges. Contextual factors are crucial as adults in caring relationships with young people make most of the important decisions about their lives. This meant that adapting PCOMS approaches to working with children and families needed to also incorporate the evidence related to the role of wider contextual factors (the extra-therapeutic factors). The approach that lies at the heart of OO-CAMHS builds on a philosophy that is 'Client Directed Outcome Informed' (CDOI) (Duncan et al, 2010). Any interaction with patients can be patient-directed and outcome-informed when the patient's voice is privileged, social justice is embraced, recovery is expected, and helpers purposefully form partnerships to: (1) enhance the factors across theories that account for success – the so-called common factors of change; (2) use patient's ideas and preferences (theories) to guide choice of technique and model; and (3) inform the work with reliable and valid measures of the patient's experience of the alliance and outcome (Duncan & Sparks, 2010).

The OO-CAMHS model has been developed and implemented in a community CAMHS team in Lincolnshire. It won an East Midlands Regional Innovation Fund award in November 2010 to help develop the model and eventually implement it across Lincolnshire CAMHS. Part of the model includes obtaining session-by-session ratings of the young person's progress (as perceived by the young person themselves and/or their parents/carers). This is done on the Outcome Rating Scale (ORS) and the Child Outcome Rating Scale (CORS). OO-CAMHS also includes the young person and/or their parent or carer giving session-by-session ratings of their experience of treatment. This is done at the end of each session using the Session Rating Scale (SRS) or the Child Session Rating Scale (CSRS).

However, the model is not limited to or by the importance of obtaining good outcome and alliance data. Because of the salience of context, work aimed at exclusively influencing the individual is the exception rather than the rule and most clinicians also have to deal with pressures from the 'system' around the 'identified' patient. So in addition to session by session measurement of outcome and alliance, OO-CAMHS involves examining the system around the young person and team dynamics resulting in 'CORE' guiding principles of: Consultation, Outcome, Relationship and Ethics of care (see **'Quick Start Guide'** pages 1 – 6 and **'Clinical Applications'** pages 40 – 91).

We believe OO-CAMHS has considerable advantages over other available whole service models (such as CAPA and CYP-IAPT) and outcome measurement projects (such as CORC). It makes active use of the evidence base, is not afraid to challenge 'norms' that have not delivered improved services, explicitly aims to change things simultaneously at several levels from the therapeutic encounter to team dynamics, builds on evidence from both RCTs and real life services that have succeeded in improving outcomes and efficiency over traditional approaches, costs a small amount to implement, doesn't need large amounts of time for training, uses simple ideas and processes that are easy to incorporate into clinical practice, and for a small amount of time and expense should result in genuinely transformed more effective, thoughtful, and efficient services.

## The Outcome and Session Rating Scales

**This section will cover:**

- An introduction to the child and adult versions of Outcome Rating Scale (ORS) and Session Rating Scale (SRS).

- The evidence base supporting the validity, reliability and clinical effectiveness of using the ORS and SRS.

- An introduction to using the ORS and SRS in clinical practice.

- An introduction to scoring and graphing the rating scales.

The Outcome Rating Scale (ORS) and Session Rating Scales (SRS) are very brief, feasible measures for tracking patient wellbeing and the quality of the therapeutic alliance, often taking less than a minute each for patients to complete and for clinicians to score and interpret. The ORS has been shown to be sensitive to change among those receiving mental health services. Numerous studies have documented concurrent, discriminative, criterion-related and predictive validity, test-retest reliability and internal-consistency reliability for the ORS and SRS (e.g. Anker et al, 2009; Bringhurst et al, 2006; Campbell & Hemsley, 2009; Duncan et al, 2003; Duncan et al, 2006; Miller et al, 2003; Reese et al, 2009). In those studies the ORS and SRS show moderately strong concurrent validity with longer, more established measures of treatment outcome and therapeutic alliance.

Feasibility (i.e. the ease and speed with which it can be explained, completed, and interpreted) of the ORS and SRS is high as they are ultra brief. As a result clinicians and patients don't mind using them and so their utilization rates are higher than other measures (Miller et al, 2003; Duncan et al, 2003). If session by session measures do not meet the time demands of real clinical practice, clinicians and patients alike may use them with reluctance at best, and resistance at worse. Much of the fear and loathing involved with doing session by session measures is not as strong with the Outcome and Session Ratings Scales as they often take only a minute or two for administration and scoring. Randomized Controlled Trials, support the efficacy of using the ORS and SRS as a patient feedback intervention across various treatment approaches (Miller et al, 2006; Anker et al, 2009; Reese et al, 2009; 2010).

The ORS, unlike many other measures, is not designed to assess what diagnosis a young person is likely to have, as it is not a symptom based measure. The ORS/ CORS is a generic measure of distress and impairment and provides clinicians with a simple tool to measure whether the intervention is associated with any meaningful (to the person) changes in that distress/impairment. This fits with research that finds that people on the whole do not seek, stay, or end services to deal with symptoms per se, but rather when those symptoms impact on functioning (Lambert, 2004). In addition other existing measures do not provide session by session predictive trajectories.

The ORS and SRS are designed and normed for adults and adolescents (ages 13+). The Children's Outcome Rating Scale (CORS) and Children's Session Rating Scale (CSRS) has been normed for ages 8-12.

There are paper versions, which are free for individual users to download and use (follow links to ORS/SRS on **www.heartandsoulofchange.com** or **www.oocamhs.com**) and web-based programmes such as '© MyOutcomes 2012' (see below and **www.myoutcomes.com**) where the patient uses the click of a mouse to input onto the ORS/CORS and SRS/CSRS. The computer-based applications allow you to administer, score, and aggregate data from the ORS/CORS and SRS/CSRS on your computer or tablet (e.g. iPad).

When downloading paper copies of the ORS/CORS and SRS/CSRS for hand-scoring, you should first be certain that the lines are 10 centimetres (10 cm) in length before printing copies for use in clinical practice.

# Outcome Rating Scale (ORS)

Looking back over the last week, including today, help us understand how you have been feeling by rating how well you have been doing in the following areas of your life, where marks to the left represent low levels and marks to the right indicate high levels. *If you are filling out this form for another person, please fill out according to how you think he or she is doing.*

**Individually**
(Personal well-being)

I----------------------------------------------------------I

**Interpersonally**
(Family, close relationships)

I----------------------------------------------------------I

**Socially**
(Work, school, friendships)

I----------------------------------------------------------I

**Overall**
(General sense of well-being)

I----------------------------------------------------------I

The Heart and Soul of Change Project

www.heartandsoulofchange.com

© 2000, Scott D. Miller and Barry L. Duncan

The ORS uses four questions so the patient can rate how they are doing Individually, Interpersonally, Socially, and Overall. Each line is 10 centimetres long and the patient makes a mark on the line, which represents how they are currently feeling and functioning; to the right as you look at the ORS, the better things are and to the left the worse things are. The first item on the ORS asks the person about how they are doing in their intrapersonal well-being (in themselves), the second how they are doing in close/family relationships, the third how they are doing socially (school, work, friendships), and the final item is for how they perceive themselves to be doing overall.

How are you doing? How are things going in your life? Please make a mark on the scale to let us know. The closer to the smiley face, the better things are. The closer to the frowny face, things are not so good.

**Me**

(How am I doing?)

**Children's Outcome Rating Scale (CORS)**

**Family**

(How are things in my family?)

**School**

(How am I doing at school?)

**Everything**

(How is everything going?)

The CORS is the same as the ORS, but uses simpler language and visual prompts using a smiley face (meaning doing well) or frowny face (meaning doing badly). On the CORS, like the ORS, to the right (smiley face) the better things are and to the left (frowny face) the worse things are.

Each line on the ORS or CORS is then scored out of 10. The 4 scores are then added up giving a total score out of 40. On the web based system these calculations are done automatically, on the paper version the clinician can manually measure the location of the mark using a ruler and calculate the total score.

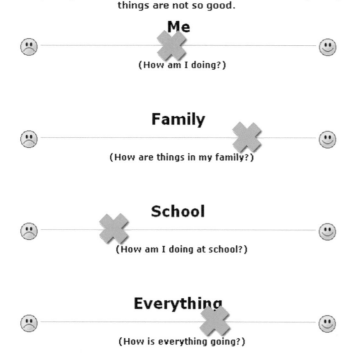

How are you doing? How are things going in your life? Please make a mark on the scale to let us know. The closer to the smiley face, the better things are. The closer to the frowny face, things are not so good.

**Me**

(How am I doing?)

**Family**

(How are things in my family?)

**School**

(How am I doing at school?)

**Everything**

(How is everything going?)

**CORS with young person's markings**

In the example above, using a ruler to measure, a score of 5 is given for 'me', 7 for 'family', 3 for 'School', and 6 for 'Everything'. The total CORS score would be 21.

The ORS is taken at the start of every session allowing the clinician to monitor an individual's progress over subsequent sessions. ORS scores are then plotted onto a graph to allow the patient and the clinician to see a visual representation of this progress session by session. In this example, the patient scored a total of 17.7 at their initial assessment and in their last session (session eight) they scored 32.4.

**Example of graph of ORS scores**

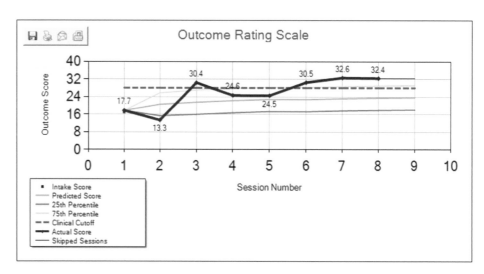

### Clinical Cut-off of the ORS:

Determining the clinical cut-off for an outcome measure accomplishes two related objectives: it provides a guide on the boundary between the non-clinical and clinical range of distress; and it provides a reference point for evaluating the severity of distress for a particular patient or patient sample.

Using the method described by Jacobson & Truax (1991), the clinical cut-off for the ORS was determined to be 25 (Miller et al, 2003). The sample on which this score is based is quite large (n=34,790) and comparison with other well-established measures shows it to be a reasonable differentiator between 'normal' and 'clinical' levels of distress. Miller and colleagues have reported that between 25-33% of people presenting for treatment score above the clinical cut-off on the ORS at intake (Miller & Duncan, 2000; Miller et al, 2005). While the clinical cut-off for adults is 25, younger patients tend to score themselves higher. The clinical cut-off for adolescents (age 13-18) is 28, and for children (age 8-12) the cut-off is 32.

### The Reliable Change Index:

When treatment is successful, scores on the ORS should increase over time. To be able to attribute such changes to factors other than normal variation in people's scoring, the difference between any two scores must exceed a statistical index known as the reliable change index (RCI). With regard to the ORS, the RCI is 5 points (Miller et al, 2003). In other words if there is a change of 5 points or more on the total of the ORS score when compared to the last or previous ORS scores, it is likely that such a change reflects that some clinically significant change has happened.

### Trajectories of Change:

In addition to the clinical cut-off, clinicians can receive feedback comparing a patient's score on the ORS to a computer-generated 'expected treatment response' (ETR) for that session number. Using a large and diverse normative sample that included 300,000 plus administrations of the ORS, Miller et al. (2004) produced algorithms capable of plotting an average trajectory of change over time based on a person's initial score on the ORS. The ETR gives the clinician and patient the chance to assess if the outcome of the treatment is similar to the average trend of change across a very large number of people. This helps quickly identify those at increased risk for a null or negative outcome so that the clinician and patient can discuss and if necessary change the treatment on offer. Clinicians can access the ETR algorithms on computer-based applications such as '© MyOutcomes 2012'.

### Limitations:

It should be remembered the ORS/CORS is a tool for clinicians and patients to understand whether patients are experiencing meaningful change during an intervention. Those with a research orientation will correctly point to its limited psychometric strength. An ultra-brief, 4-question measure will inevitably have a poorer psychometric profile compared to longer questionnaires. Undoubtedly its strength is feasibility in the clinical setting and as long as it is understood that the ORS/CORS is a measure of generic change in perceived distress/impairment, its psychometric properties are more than 'good enough' for this purpose. Another limitation is lack of 'anchor points'. An analogue scale with no accompanying descriptors for what a mark on a line means, results in limited capacity for comparisons across different presentations/symptom profiles. This means it works best as a comparator for the patient's own ratings, rather than between patients. In some ways this can also be viewed as a strength as although a 3 out of 10 (for example) on intrapersonal may be one persons rating for something an observer may consider 'mild' and another's 3 on that scale would be considered as 'severe' by the same observer, the point of reference is always what that score means to the person doing the rating not the observer. A final limitation worth mentioning is that younger children tend to rate in a more 'black and white' manner due to less developed cognitive discrimination. This can mean that younger children's ratings are more likely to be very high/low or in the middle.

Thus for some children, their parents/carers ratings of them may provide a more discriminating measure of whether change is occurring.

# The SRS and CSRS

The Session Rating Scale (SRS) and Child Session Rating Scale (CSRS) is a measure of the therapeutic alliance between the patient and clinician. Like the ORS the SRS utilizes four questions, but is given at the end of a session.

It asks for the yp/p/c rating in 4 areas: Did they feel like they were listened to, understood and respected; did they feel that they got to talk and work on what they wanted to; was the therapist approach one that suited them; and how they thought the session went overall.

Scoring for SRS and CSRS is identical to that of the ORS; four 10 centimetre lines on which the patient marks where they feel appropriate, giving a total score out of 40.

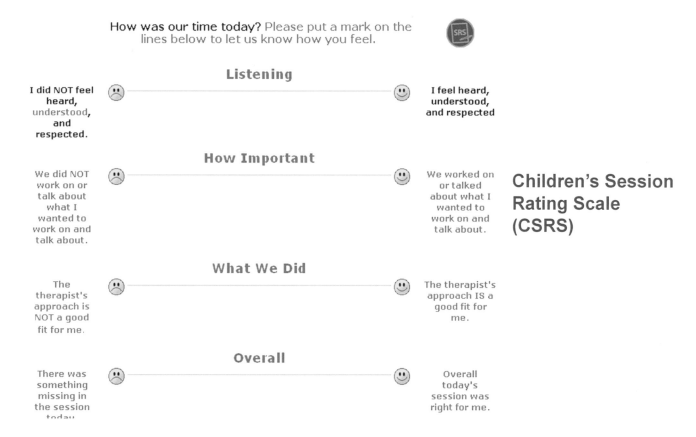

Scores on the SRS/CSRS are plotted on a graph showing session by session ratings. The patient and the clinician can then monitor the progress of their relationship, identifying immediately if there are any problems.

If there is a score below 36 overall or below 9 out of 10 on any item, then this is a prompt to discuss with the yp/p/c whether there is anything that could be done differently to help improve their experience.

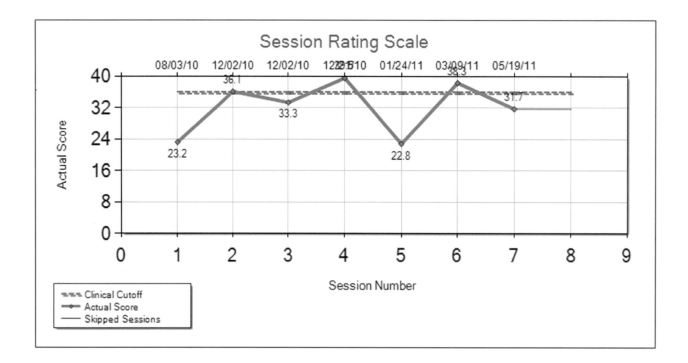

For further information on using the ORS/CORS and SRS/CSRS in clinical practice please see section on **'OO Sessions'** (pages 49 – 70).

# Using © MyOutcomes 2012

MyOutcomes (www.myoutcomes.com) is the practical web-based application of the Patient-Directed Outcome-Informed (CDOI) clinical approach. CDOI is based on the idea that patient feedback can improve effectiveness by tailoring therapy to patient's preferences and needs. This approach helps foster a strong patient-provider alliance. It is an on-line programme that charges an annual fee for each user and is based around ratings on the ORS/CORS and SRS/CSRS.

## A typical session using MyOutcomes

Immediately before/at the start of each session, a patient takes about a minute to complete the 4-item Outcomes Rating Scale (ORS). Near the end of each session, patients take about a minute to complete the Session Rating Scale (SRS). MyOutcomes provides feedback to the patient and clinician about how well the patient is following the expected trajectory. It warns if a patient is at risk for dropout or other negative outcomes. MyOutcomes encourages conversations between patient and clinician. This helps the clinician fine-tune the treatment to meet the specific needs and preferences of the patient and helps give the patient a greater voice in the recovery process.

You can set up the treatment episode to rate not only the young person, but also one, two or more other feedback sources (such as the parents or carers). This enables you to track the ratings on the ORS of others such as the parents as well as or instead of the young person.

### Administering the ORS/CORS and SRS/CSRS using MyOutcomes

**At the start of the session:**

1. **Locate and click the patient's record to display the patient tools page.**

2. **Administer ORS: Click the ORS icon to administer the Outcomes Rating Scale.**

> ***Paper Version Option:*** Click the Paper ORS icon to manually transfer ORS scores from a paper version of the ORS to MyOutcomes.

3. **Complete the ORS: Ask patient to make sure to click the check-mark icon to save the survey results:** MyOutcomes generates empirically based feedback messages that encourage discussions between providers and patients about their treatment.

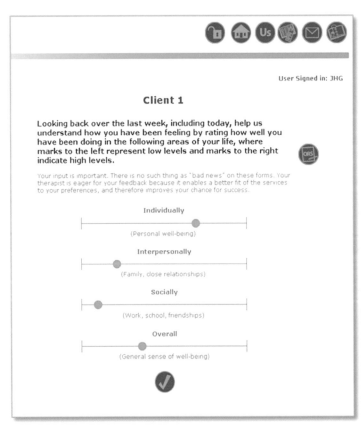

**Before the end of the session:**

4. **Administer SRS: Click the SRS icon to administer the Session Rating Scale.**

> ***Paper Version Option:***  Click on the Paper SRS icon to manually transfer scores from a paper version of the SRS.

5. **Complete the SRS: Ask the patient to make sure to click the check-mark icon to save the survey results:** MyOutcomes generates empirically based feedback messages that stimulate constructive discussion between providers and patients about the strength of their alliance.

The ORS or CORS, administered at the start of every session, assesses the patient's rating of progress in response to the treatment that is being delivered. It compares the patient's scores to an expected trajectory of change that is based on a database of more than 300,000 administrations.

**00000002D**

**Most Recent Feedback Messages**

**Results:**
You are reporting a great deal of progress since the last visit.

**Activity:**
Explore: (1) what you are doing to make progress possible; (2) how you can build on and continue your success; and (3) any concerns you have about maintaining progress. Consider whether longer time between visits will build your confidence. Do not be surprised if the pace of change slows or a minor setback occurs.

Individually: 7.1 out of 10

Interpersonally: 7.8 out of 10

Socially: 8.1 out of 10

Overall: 5.0 out of 10

Total Score: 28.0

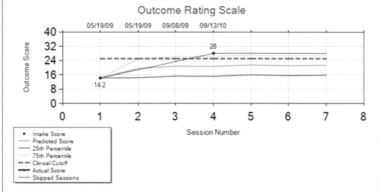

Results are immediately graphed and presented along with an explanation of results, suggested activities, and a green, yellow, or red hand indicating the general direction of therapy, whether it is heading in the right direction, needs to be tailored, or may require a change of direction.

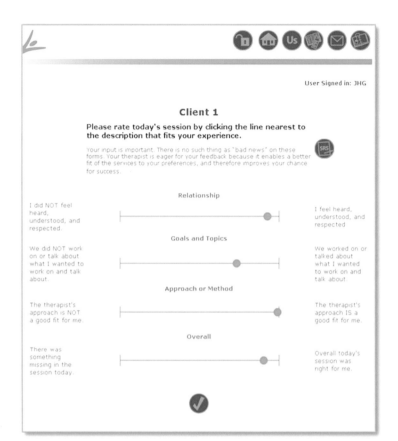

The SRS or CSRS, given near the end of each session, assesses the patient's perception of his or her alliance with the provider. Research demonstrates that a patient's progress and the therapeutic alliance can be used to determine the appropriateness of the current treatment, assess the need for further treatment, and suggest clinical consultation for patients who are not progressing at expected rates.

A graph compares the patient's rating of the alliance to typical patient's responses, highlighting results that fall in the bottom quartile of all responses in order to alert the patient and therapists to a possible at-risk relationship. Feedback messages highlight areas of the relationship that receive particularly low marks and encourage proactive discussion of steps that can repair the relationship.

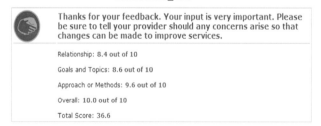

00000002D_CT1

Thanks for your feedback. Your input is very important. Please be sure to tell your provider should any concerns arise so that changes can be made to improve services.

Relationship: 8.4 out of 10

Goals and Topics: 8.6 out of 10

Approach or Methods: 9.6 out of 10

Overall: 10.0 out of 10

Total Score: 36.6

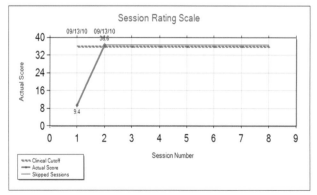

# Putting the OO into the CAMHS Team

> **This section will cover:**
>
> - The most important factors associated with successful service transformation projects.
>
> - A detailed overview of the CORE principles of OO-CAMHS.

OO-CAMHS is a UK implementation of the Heart and Soul of Change Project's Partners for Change Outcome Management System (PCOMS) (Duncan, 2012). It is a whole service model that incorporates existing evidence on how to improve outcomes, reduce DNAs and dropout rates and save money through improved therapeutic efficiency. The CORE guiding principles of the OO-CAHMS approach have been covered in the Quick Start guide and are Consultation, Outcome, Relationship and Ethics of care.

There is a balancing act to be achieved between so-called 'model fidelity' (the degree a team adheres to the principles) and the spirit of this model, which creates a tension with the concept of model fidelity. OO-CAMHS is trying to encourage an open learning system in the therapeutic encounter, where practitioners are learning to develop in an open and flexible manner, adjusting their approach in response to feedback, with this being more important than model fidelity in the approach they use. We therefore hope that OO teams will be more concerned with how they develop cultures of inclusion and learning from feedback and each other and this will trump 'model fidelity' (including to the OO principles). Confident but flexible, reflective, and validating clinicians are more likely to emerge from similarly confident, reflective, and validating teams. Viewed from this perspective, well functioning OO-teams should expect to have on-going reflection on practice, which may result in on-going changes and new ideas/approaches being introduced.

Teams like practitioners need to find their feet, develop their identities, and understand what they are good at and what they may need to work on. Like good therapy, good teams should have a freedom to innovate and take therapeutic risks and that means sometimes doing things differently to other teams. We encourage this sort of diversity rather than stifle it by insistence on 'model fidelity', providing there is evidence to show that innovations are making meaningful and positive differences. If a team is demonstrating good outcomes (such as good effect sizes of change, low number of onward referrals, reduction in number of long term patients with no evidence of improvements, low rates of DNA etc.) then in our opinion it is an OO team and we should seek to learn from them.

However 3 factors have emerged as being of particular importance in those teams that have successfully implemented service transformation projects that have worked. It should be stated that these 3 factors are based largely on experiential/ qualitative feedback (e.g. from successful/unsuccessful PCOMS projects). The 3 factors are:

1. Clinician buy in,

2. Data management,

3. Data integrity.

## The 3 factors associated with successful implementation and service transformation

### Clinician 'buy in':

Many feedback and outcome projects fail due to lack of engagement with clinicians. As highlighted under **'The OO-CAMHS Project'** (pages 19 – 25). this has been a problem with CORC and CAPA and could also be problematic with CYP-IAPT. Problems leading to lack of engagement include the cumbersome nature of rating scales used (lack of feasibility), and ideological objections. Whilst it will never be possible to persuade all practitioners of the merits of service transformation focussed on outcomes, we believe the OO-CAMHS model is more clinician friendly (though accept its ideological position won't be to everyone's liking) and more flexible than many other models. Not only are the rating scales easy to use and the most feasible of any rating scales we have come across, but its lack of technical model 'allegiance' means that as an ideology it values diversity and is not interested in the 'brand wars', rather sees a place for all the different skills that differently trained clinicians bring.

### Data management:

An understandable concern relates to the data generated on personal outcomes of each clinician. The concern is that clinicians will be ranked in 'league tables', with managers then deciding to focus on or even make redundant those at the bottom of this table. However, we recognise differential efficacy may relate to dealing with groups who have different severity or complexity and so we may end up comparing apples with oranges. Individual clinician outcome data should be for use in supervision and sometimes team meetings to help understand clinical and clinician needs and should never be used by higher management as a way of comparing individual clinician outcomes. Maintaining clarity about data management and keeping the individualised clinician data 'out of reach' of higher management is therefore essential. Clinicians' looking over their shoulder in a persecutory environment is not conducive to improved team performance.

A concentration, particularly in supervision and in the early weeks and months of an OO project, on getting all the clinicians in the habit of incorporating feedback (such as using the ORS and SRS) into every (or nearly every) session, so that the team is producing a complete dataset (particularly for all new patients) as soon as possible has been found to be associated with successful service transformation projects. Making explicit an understanding to everyone that this is the process and then helping everyone adjust and learn from there once they have properly given it a go, seems important. Teams able to get a full (or nearly full) dataset as soon as possible are more likely to succeed than the more 'organic' approach of waiting for people to try it.

## Consultation:

40-85% of variance of outcome is accounted for by extra-therapeutic factors such as social support, parental mental health, socioeconomic status and motivation. This should make us take seriously the de-centring of our (and our treatments) importance to the process of change.

### Ideas to consider:

Before embarking on treatment think about the external factors/system around the child. Remember complex cases can often be created by over-intervention that distances people from their existing strengths, abilities and resilience and instead re-enforces feelings of vulnerability and lack of coping.

Aim for not more than one agency working on any one problem at any one time. Use professionals meetings when one agency or more are already involved with the problem/issue the young person has been referred for.

Think about who already has an attachment or important relationship with the young person, particularly when that person already has other agencies involved in their care. For example young people in the care system may already have a good relationship with someone in a caring relationship with them (such as a care worker in a children's home). Supporting and advising that person(s) may prove more beneficial than starting a new therapy process.

Consider who has the motivation to change. Is it the young person who wants change, their parents, teachers etc.? For example if it is mainly teachers it may be better to meet with representatives from school first.

Try to establish whether there is a stable predictable set of circumstances before embarking on treatment. For example on-going legal disputes, custody battles, messy separations, and unstable placements are likely to make individual therapeutic interventions secondary in importance. First try and help those involved establish a safe, stable and predictable environment.

The dynamics that occur between agencies can also occur within them. This means that careful co-ordination should take place if more than one clinician from the Multi-Disciplinary Team is working on treating the problem. As a general rule, aim for one clinician at a time being involved with treatment. This clinician will be aiming to develop an alliance from their first meeting and all being well progress will be made and no other clinician will need to be involved. If no progress is made or it becomes clear from the first meeting that the patient needs to be reviewed by someone else in the team (for example, the psychiatrist) then that is the time to involve another clinician. Avoid more than one clinician working simultaneously and separately with a young person and/or parent/carer (yp/p/c). As is the case with agencies, this can lead to unnecessary confusion, duplication, and give potentially undermining (to personal strengths and resources) messages about severity and capacity for recovery.

Think carefully before offering intensive treatment packages to families in crisis. Over-intervention (e.g. daily phone calls etc.) at crisis points can inadvertently re-enforce a lack of ability of families to find solutions and over-emphasise the importance of our treatments. Help families think about what they can do to get through the crisis such as their own sources of extra support, but resist temptation to provide immediate packages of treatment. It may prove more effective to wait until the crisis is resolved or attenuated, before a treatment package is offered. The task is containing the high emotions while the yp/p/c work through a crisis.

## Outcomes:

Session by session monitoring of outcomes with regular feedback to the patient of how they are progressing can by itself improve the outcome. If the outcome is showing no signs of improvement after 3-6 sessions, there is a high risk of a poor outcome. In psychiatric disorders, change as a result of an intervention usually starts to happen early in treatment for the majority. Matching the treatment model to a diagnostic category has a relatively small impact on outcome.

*Remember: the young person will fill the ORS/CORS about themselves, and the parents/carers will fill in the ORS about their perception of how they believe their child is doing.*

### Ideas to consider:

Provide on-going feedback, session by session, using Patient Related Outcome Measures (PROMs). Make sure the measure is simple and feasible otherwise it will not engage clinicians. OO-CAMHS recommends the Outcome Rating Scale (ORS) and Child Outcome Rating Scale (CORS). These have good psychometric properties and are easy to incorporate into clinical practice as they only take a minute or two for the patient to complete (see **'The Outcome and Session Rating Scales'**, pages 26 - 34).

Keep the service focussed more on providing treatment to improve outcomes rather than assessments (such as diagnostic ones) that are detached from impairment or a focus on what the service may be able to help change.

Engagement with services and therapeutic relationships start from the first meeting. Where possible avoid separating the process of assessment from treatment such as allocating different clinicians to do the assessment than the treatment (as sometimes happens in the CAPA model). Try and match the clinician to the patient from the first session. Patients and their families find it hard to keep changing clinicians as they often have to repeat their story.

Find out who has the motivation to change based on the ORS/CORS scores. This will help decide whether to focus treatment on the young person, his/her parents, or both.

Ask the yp/p/c to rate the ORS/CORS in a way that is relevant to his or her decision to seek treatment because you want the measure to reflect progress in that area.

The ORS/CORS can be used to help structure the assessment session. As yp/p/c fill in the 4 questions, asking them why they put their marks where they did can lead to a conversation that connects their mark on the ORS/CORS to the aspects of the presenting problem they are most concerned about.

Low scores on one of the questions on the ORS/CORS can identify areas in which the yp/p/c are looking for change, whereas high scores can point toward competencies, resources, and social supports. Low scores may also point to areas of risk that may need further exploration (e.g. low score on intra-personal dimension may lead to exploring low mood and suicidal ideation). However, also take particular note of and highlight any strengths, competencies, or resources the yp/p/c have. This can also help with managing any risk.

If the young person and/or their parents rate above the cut off for clinically significant impairment on the ORS/CORS, discuss whether they are there because they have been told to come (e.g. by school, GP, social services) but are not particularly motivated to seek treatment, or whether there is a specific issue they wish to address (such as a specific phobia, or a concern about future problems), but overall this is not affecting their day to day functioning. This will help you arrive at a decision together about the likely benefit (or lack of benefit) they may get from further treatment.

Use the PROM actively to help shape the intervention. For example, if the ORS is indicating that family relationships are the biggest area of concern, discuss whether this is what the yp/p/c want to address in the sessions/treatment plan.

Keep a record of the outcome score session by session and plot a graph to show progress session by session. Discuss the progress shown on the graph at the beginning of each session with the yp/p/c, to check that it matches their perceptions (e.g. "*According to your ratings, things look like they've improved since we last met, does that sound right to you?*"). Computer based systems such as '© MyOutcomes 2012' automatically produce a graph after the patient fills in the ORS/CORS on-line.

**If no improvement has occurred after 5 sessions discuss with the yp/p/c and/ or the Multidisciplinary team**. Consider: change of therapeutic approach, change of therapist, agreeing a deadline with the young person and/or their parent/carer after which a change in approach/therapist will be tried if there continues to be no change. Avoid getting stuck in long-term treatment with no accompanying improvement. The idea of the 5 session review is to keep a process of regular review alive so that you don't 'drift' unthinkingly into a long term treatment without any evidence that such a process is helping the young person.

If after changes of approach and therapist there continues to be no change, discuss with the supervisor and then yp/p/c, the possibility that the service is not the right one for them or perhaps this is not the right time. Reflect on possible alternative services or the possibility that treatment may be better given at a different point in time (for example when circumstances are more stable and predictable).

Once the yp/p/c are scoring above the cut-off for clinical significance (i.e. are rating that there is no longer clinically significant impairment), or their scores have reached a plateau (for 2 or 3 sessions at least) after a period of improvement, discuss discharge options such as discharging back to the GP, arranging a review appointment several months later and then discharge if all is still going well, or not making another appointment but keeping notes open for a number of months and then discharge if all continues to be well. Leave the choice with the yp/p/c. If they still wish for regular appointments, agree how many or for what time frame before discharge if all continues to be well. Using a system of formal graphed feedback enables early recognition of when an intervention is likely to have achieved what it set out to achieve and encourages a discussion about discharge sooner rather than later.

When patients have reached a plateau on the graph (suggesting they have reached the maximum benefit they will derive from treatment), but are reluctant to leave; help them with planning for community connection and continued recovery outside of treatment. This could mean just reducing the frequency of meetings and continuing to monitor their goals. However, others may find it helpful to think about supports in the community including family, friends, and other organisations. Consequently, it is also useful to include an orientation toward 'recovery' thinking. This simply means conveying the attitude that there is a beginning and end to therapy, and that recovery is a life-long journey that can continue outside of treatment.

Maintenance of change after treatment is associated with patients ascribing the change to something they did. As change happens, clinicians can focus on what the yp/p/c did, not on what they (the clinician) did. The clinician can provide possible pathways to go down that may help, but it is the patient who will do the walking. Even if patients attribute change to professional expertise, or a medication, they can still be asked to consider how they took advantage of what was offered by others; what qualities the intervention brought out in them; what they did to use the changes to their benefit; and what they will do in the future to ensure their gains remain in place. The process of de-centring the clinician also means that patients are given the responsibility for changing and for bringing about the changes they achieve.

# Relationship

Alliance as rated by the patient is by far the strongest factor, from those within treatment, associated with improved outcomes.

Developing strong therapeutic alliances is key to the OO-CAMHS approach. This means more than just empathy, warmth, and genuineness (important as these are). Meaningful relationships also include agreeing on the models of understanding used and goals of the treatment. A capacity to be flexible with how a problem is to be understood and possible solutions discovered is important, particularly when there is a large difference between the cultural beliefs and values of the patient and clinician. Mental health services have a poor track record of engaging those from ethnic minority communities. Greater openness to models of meaning that are not derived from the dominant culture can thus assist in improving the chances of meaningful engagement.

## Ideas to consider:

Opportunities to develop an alliance start from the first meeting. Models that include a triage with someone other than the clinician who does the assessment subsequently offering treatment could turn out to be a missed opportunity that introduces unnecessary inefficiency for the service and frustration for the service user. Aim to have the assessment appointment conducted by a clinician who can continue to meet with the yp/p/c should further treatment be offered.

Measure the alliance at the end of each session. Make sure the measure is simple and feasible otherwise it will not engage clinicians. OO-CAMHS recommends the Session Rating Scale (SRS) and Child Session Rating Scale (CSRS). These have good psychometric properties and only take a minute or two for the patient to complete (see **'The Outcome and Session Rating Scales'**, pages 26 - 34).

From the first session create a culture of strong interest in patient feedback. Building strong alliances is important particularly early in treatment.

Use the alliance measure as a formal tool to get patient feedback. Patients are often reluctant to highlight problems or issues they have if simply invited to comment on how they experience the session.

Briefly go through the SRS even if the score on the SRS/CSRS is above 36. This could be as simple as asking "*Is there anything that comes to mind as you were rating the session that you would like us to address next time, or anything that you thought would be better if I did differently?*"

Look for subtle clues when they rate their experience of the session. For example if a yp/p/c marks 9.9 out of 10 (on the SRS) on being listened to and treated with respect, on the approach used and on the session overall but 9.7 out of 10 on talking about or working on the issues they wanted to talk about/work on; treat this as an invitation to discuss whether there was something else they wanted to talk about/ work on, despite the very high overall ratings.

If the score on the SRS/CSRS is below 36, talk to the person and ask for their help in understanding what didn't work as well as they may have hoped and to help you understand what they would like you to change about your approach, model, or goals.

Always address and discuss alliance issues before the yp/p/c leaves the session. This is often simply to make a plan on how you intend to address any issues raised the next time you meet. Avoid leaving any alliance issues that have come up, un-discussed.

There is no bad news from feedback. It is not a measure of clinician competence or anything else negative about the clinician or patient. It is about the fit of the service/ relationship. Unless you really show that you want the negative feedback, you are unlikely to get it and you may loose valuable opportunities to learn from patients what is most important to them in treatment.

Talking about the relationship is hard and building a culture of feedback takes a concerted effort. Don't expect too much but recognize that your authentic attention to the alliance via a tool like the SRS helps to build good partnerships. Remember scores on the SRS are not as important as talking about their meaning.

# Ethics of Care

Team effects are often found in outcome studies. Using the database associated with the ORS/CORS results, means there is clinician-by-clinician outcome data available. If this is not handled sensitively it can become a source of anxiety for clinicians rather than a source of empowerment. A clinician anxious about their place in a team is more likely to perform poorly.

Ideas to consider:

Putting patients' strengths, abilities and choices in the centre of the therapeutic process needs clinicians who similarly feel empowered by having their strengths, abilities and therapeutic choices noticed and respected. The OO-CAMHS approach involves building strong relationships with patients, which is mirrored by building strong relationships in the team.

Strong team relationships makes it easier to 'fail successfully' as a clinician, and pass the patient who is not improving in treatment with one member of the team to another clinician in that team.

Just like each patient is different and makes different choices and has a different profile of strengths and challenges, so each clinician is different. Team consultants, managers and supervisors have an important role in noticing and re-enforcing each individual clinician's strengths and helping them develop their therapeutic skills through that clinician's choices.

As team relationships develop so an understanding of what each clinician is good at develops. This is unlikely to be condition specific or even profession specific and more likely to be personality and skills based. For example "*Colin is great where a firm non nonsense approach is helpful, Philomena has a fantastic knack of engaging 'stroppy adolescents', Ted has developed great skills in working with schools to get teachers to think about adjusting their approach, Karen is wonderful in providing structured stage by stage interventions, Katie's compassion and skill building works fantastically with kids who have little self-confidence, Iram has an ability to build bridges between adolescents who self harm and their South Asian parents, Wayne knows how to engage parents who feel they've 'tried everything' in thinking about parenting approaches afresh etc."* This more personal connection to and understanding of clinician's skills, reflects the centrality of meaningful relationships in mental health work.

Building relationships is an on-going process. Make regular opportunities to do things together such as weekly case discussion forums, running groups together, regular team development days which can be academic/new service developments/team reflection, and creating simple social opportunities such as team lunches (and not just at Christmas!).

Use the outcome data in supervision and the overall whole team outcome data in team meetings. This generally provides positive re-enforcement as clinicians and teams can see that they are making a positive difference.

Get feedback from service users on how to improve services. This could be from young people, parents, carers, other professionals, and using informal or formal means.

Develop robust supervisory structures to incorporate outcome feedback scores as a routine in supervision. Similarly, get into the habit of discussing outcome scores during any case discussion such as discussing cases in a team/peer supervision meeting.

Good therapy sees positive value, strengths, acceptance, and abilities in their patients. Good teams see positive value, strengths, acceptance and abilities in their clinicians. Team consultants, managers and supervisors have an important role in noticing and re-enforcing each individual clinician's strengths and helping them develop their therapeutic skills through that clinician's choices.

DO NOT strive for a one-size fits all approach for teams. The idea that 'model fidelity' is essential can result in alienating clinicians and leave a team vulnerable to feeling a system is being imposed before clinicians have had an experience of positive change. As we highlight above, there is a difficult balance to be struck as one of the factors associates with successful service transformation projects is 'data integrity', which means getting clinicians to use rating scales as quickly as possible. Use of data also needs clarifying with clinicians before adopting OO-CAMHS. Outcome data should NEVER be used to compare clinicians in a league table of outcomes. Any team that has decided to use data in this manner is not an OO-CAMHS team and cannot be part of a project to improve outcomes for all.

# OO Sessions

**This section will cover:**

- A comprehensive overview of the service experience for patients from referral to discharge.

- Detailed examples of using and interpreting the rating scales in clinical practice.

- Examples of words and phrases that can be used when discussing rating scales, progress, lack of progress and discharge.

## Coming to CAMHS

It is likely that the young person and their family have already completed a great deal of therapeutic processing before they enter the clinic for their initial assessment appointment. After all there needs to be recognition that there is a problem and that this problem is going to require the kind of help that is beyond the resources of the family and the system around them. In addition, for a specialist mental health service to be involved it is likely that a referral will have been made, which will require the young person and/or family to visit an entry point of care, (such as the GP) to discuss their problems.

We should not under-estimate how much motivation and commitment may be required to attend this first appointment and 'talk' about the issues. Many parents will already be feeling guilty, fearing that they may have done something wrong or that they may get blamed for their child's difficulty by the professional they see. The young person may have to take time off from their schooling; the family member/carer may have to make arrangements for leave from work, not to mention orientating themselves to the clinic building to arrive and find the right place for the correct time. The relationship that the clinician has with this new family will have already started to set its foundations before the family arrives on the day. Efforts made to accommodate the wishes of the young person and their family, from being flexible about the appointment date to sending directions to the clinic, all begin to set up the relationship they will have with the service and subsequently the clinician. Having a service with good foundations not only helps prepare the family for the initial assessment appointment, but, in addition has already 'kick-started' families to have positive expectations about the therapeutic relationship.

# Arrival at the clinic

When the young person and/or family arrive at the clinic it is time to cement the foundations of this pre-assessment relationship. People come with all sorts of thoughts about what to expect, however there are some basic aspects of healthcare appointments that people notice and that should therefore be thought about. An acknowledgement that they are expected by the clinician, that they are shown where to wait, that the place is comfortable enough, and that they have a clear indication about when they will be seen, are all things that could be easily accommodated. Appointments that take place in community clinics or hospitals may be in a medically orientated environment, which may need extra efforts to make young people feel more comfortable, help to reduce anxiety, and improve the likelihood of a positive experience when they meet the clinician. It is useful to think about the whole journey patients make before meeting the clinicians. Expectations can play a significant role in improving outcomes, so investment in preparing families for sessions and making them feel welcome on arrival is worthwhile.

# An overview of 'OO' sessions

Once patients are accepted, the acronym OUTCOME nicely captures the basics of the type of 'rituals' that become a routine part of the way you get the 'OO' into the clinical session:

Outcome Rating Scale (ORS) or Child Outcome Rating Scale (CORS) completed. Aim to complete the ORS/CORS with young person and/or parent/carer (yp/p/c) at the start of each session.

Understand the meanings behind the scores. Check out with the yp/p/c what their marks on the ORS mean, so that they have an active involvement in the process and to ensure the marks they put are a meaningful part of the treatment process.

Track the movement of the outcome scores. Make a graph of the scores from session to session (or use the computer generated graph if using an electronic system such as '© MyOutcomes 2012'). Check with the yp/p/c whether the graph of change matches their perceptions.

Change-Focused Conversation. Keep the yp/p/c involved in shaping the direction of the treatment. Discuss with them what scores they would like to change as a result of treatment.

Ongoing linking back to ORS/CORS scores. As sessions go on, clinicians can link back to the outcome scores collected and expectations for change.

Monitor the Therapeutic Relationship. Use the Session Rating Scale (SRS) or Child Session Rating Scale (CSRS) to explore what the yp/p/c thought about the session and monitor how they are rating the quality of the therapeutic relationship. Create a culture of active soliciting of patient feedback.

Engage the system. Adults make many of the most important decisions about a young person's life. This could be their parents or other professionals. Their engagement in the process is often vital. Others, not just the young person, will usually play an active part in the treatment process and their opinions, including through completing the ORS and SRS, can be crucial.

- *Outcome Rating Scale (ORS) or Child Outcome Rating Scale (CORS) completed:*

Try to avoid using clinical jargon and explain the purpose of the ORS/CORS and its rationale in a common sense way. The specific wording is not important, but aim to be clear and to say something that you understand and believe in order to enhance the genuineness with which you say it. Here are examples:

To young person and carer: *Before we get started I would be grateful if you could help me out by taking a bit of time to fill out a very brief questionnaire to help me understand how things are going for you. Every time we meet I will ask you to fill this form again as this will help us track progress and see whether what we're doing here is making a difference to you. Are you OK with that?*

Or

To young person and carer: *One of my priorities is to make sure you benefit from coming here. One way to achieve this is for you to fill in a brief questionnaire every time we meet that will help us keep an eye on your progress from session to session. I like to use two brief rating scales to help us with that – the first scale is one I'd like you to fill in at the start of our meeting. This one is about how you feel you are doing. The second is one I'll ask you to fill out at the end of the meeting. This one is about how you felt about todays meeting and any plan we made. Your feedback is a really important part of making sure whatever work we do together will be of most benefit to you. Does that all sound OK to you?*

If the young person or parent asks for clarification about one of the four subscales on the ORS/CORS, they can be explained in the following ways (adjusted depending on the age of the person):

Individually: *This means in yourself as an individual, how you're feeling inside, it's a bit like a symptoms scale rating your level of distress.*

Interpersonally: *This is about how you're getting on in your family or close personal relationships, generally speaking the people you're living with.*

Socially: *This about your life socially outside the home, which is mainly to do with how you're getting on at school and with friendships.*

Overall: *One way to think about this is to think about where you are in your life right now compared to where you expected or wanted to be.*

Scoring the ORS/CORS is done in front of the yp/p/c using a centimetre ruler (or, if using an electronic system such as '© MyOutcomes 2012' the score will automatically be generated and put on a graph). When using or making paper copies of the ORS/CORS, make sure that the lines are 10 centimetres in length. To score the ORS/CORS, determine the distance in centimetres (to the nearest millimetre, e.g., '5.4') between the left pole and the person's mark on each individual item. Add all four numbers together to obtain the total score. The score can either be plotted on a paper graph, or can be entered into one of the computer-based applications such as '© MyOutcomes 2012'. The computer-based applications allow you to administer, score, and aggregate data from the ORS and SRS directly onto your computer or tablet. The scores from the four visual analogue scales are added for an overall score with a total possible score of 40. The overall score is then plotted onto a graph.

- *Understand the meanings behind the scores:*

The ORS/CORS cut off scores between the clinical population and the non-clinical population are different depending on the age of the patient.

The cut off scores for the ORS in 13-17 year olds (self reporting and carer reporting) is 28, and for over 18s its 25. The CORS (ages 12 and under) cut off scores for a child self-reporting are 32, whilst for the carer reporting its 28.

It is important to explain the cut off scores to the young people. Having different graphs for the different age groups with the cut off score line included helps with the explanation:

To young person and carer:  *Great thanks. Let me show you what I have done. The lines on the form are each 10cm so I have scored them with a ruler, added them up and plotted them on this graph. (Young person's name) I have put your score here with a blue dot, and (parent's name) I have placed your score here with a green dot. Scores above this line* [clinical cut off line] *represent young people who seem to be plodding along all right in life and generally are not needing to seek help. Scores below this line, like yours, are typically young people who are having problems and want some help to make some changes. Is that true for you?*

*OK, so when we fill out this form each time we meet I will be putting your scores on the graph and connecting the dots, and hopefully we will soon see a line going up which will tells us we are on the right track. If it does not go up, or goes down, we will know about it right away and we can talk about it and together work out whether there's anything that might need to be different, for example with the treatment.*

It is important to help the yp/p/c connect the problems that brought them to the clinic with their ORS and CORS scores.

To young person and carer (laying out the ORS or CORS in front of them): *I would be grateful if you could tell me a bit about why you put the marks where you placed them so I can better understand the problems that brought you here.*

This will often end up with a narrative about the problem. Such discussions can be a part of your normal interviewing style and how you come up with shared formulations with patients. The only difference is linking their responses and the shared formulation to the ORS and/or CORS scores.

- *Track the movement of the outcome scores:*

The ORS is scored in the session right after the patient has filled out the form, and is plotted onto a graph. If you are using an electronic version such as '© MyOutcomes 2012' the graph will come up automatically and show how the yp/p/c score compares to the clinical cut off.

- *Change-Focused Conversation:*

You can use the scales to help establish what kind of changes and goals the yp/p/c want and any theories or preferences they may have on how to get there.

To young person or carer: *What will you and others notice that will be different when your marks on this line move from where you placed it to over here at this end nearer the smiley face? What ideas do you have about what needs to happen to move your mark from here to there* [pointing toward the smiley face]?

- *Ongoing linking back to ORS/CORS scores:*

For example:

To the young person: *It sounds like you are spending a lot of your day worrying and avoiding places out of fear, does that explain your mark here on the Me (How am I doing?) question?*

To the parent: *It sounds like there is a lot of arguing and anger amongst family members, does that explain your mark here on the Family (How are things in my family?) question? Is there anything else that helps explain your mark?*

To the teacher: *It sounds like running out of class and not knowing where he is going is your biggest concern for Kevin. Does that explain your mark here on the School (How am I doing at school?) question? Is there anything else that helps explain your mark?*

It is common for the young person and carer to have different scores on the different questions in the scale. It can be useful to explore the reasons and meanings behind these differences:

To the young person and their mother: *Ahmed, I noticed you rated how things are going in the family closer to the frowny face, and Selma (mother) you rated your son closer towards the smiley face. What do you both make of that?*

## Monitor the Therapeutic Relationship:

Clinicians who can elicit negative feedback from their patients often have a better chance of forging a more meaningful alliance. Forging a strong alliance helps yp/p/c feel safe to give honest feedback. Building a culture of feedback needs the clinician to recognize and believe in its importance.

When introducing the SRS/CSRS the position to adopt is that you highly value all feedback. Convey to patients that there is no such thing as bad feedback. All feedback is good and gives you the opportunity to make adjustments to improve the chances of getting and keeping a good outcome. Low SRS scores give you an opportunity to repair ruptures to the alliance, and make the necessary adjustments to help improve the outcome.

Ask the yp/p/c to fill in the SRS/CSRS about 5 minutes before the end of the session, to allow a bit of time to discuss any issues that may emerge and make a brief plan on how to address what has come up (for example in the next session).

To young person and carer: *We need to end soon, but before we do I would be grateful if you could fill out this brief questionnaire which asks your opinion about today's session. The feedback you give me helps me understand your opinion about today's meeting and in particular alerts us to anything that was maybe missing or didn't go quite right. The more feedback you can give the better, so please try and be as honest as you can when filling this out. Is that OK?*

The cut off score on the SRS/CSRS is 36 out of a possible 40 and so a score below 36 should be discussed. Anything below 9 on each scale should also be discussed. This is because most people tend to give positive feedback, however, the purpose of the SRS/CSRS is to encourage feedback on things that need to change/improve from the yp/p/c's perspective. As you will often be working with more than one person in a session, scoring can take a bit of time and so you can just look at the marks for any scores that are not near the right.

When scores are 36 and above: *These marks are pretty high which suggests you felt happy about how today's meeting went. Is that right? Can you think of anything at all that I might be able to do differently to make things better in any way?*

When scores are below 36 (or you notice that one scale is below 9): *That's really helpful. I'm grateful for you being honest and giving me a chance to try to make some changes. It would be really helpful to understand what you think I need to do next time for you to feel that this works better for you.*

● *Engage the system:*

Young people have some of the most important decisions about their lives made by others, usually their parents. They exist in a nest of meaningful relationships where they need to feel important and valued. Involving those who are meaningful to the young person, in the treatment process can therefore be of great value. Parents and carers often need to think about how they might change or what they can do to support their child and so can be key to a positive outcome. Often it is the parents or carers who want their child to change, whilst the young person is not so concerned. This all means that involving parents or carers either at every session or at regular intervals is potentially of great importance.

Beyond the immediate family there maybe a whole network of potentially important people and/or agencies to keep in mind. These days we have to negotiate our way through something of a maze of services each with a bewildering array of processes and bureaucracies: social services, housing, voluntary, religious, counselling, legal, education, etc. School for example makes up a big part of children's lives. There are a variety of ways to engage with schools, from picking up the phone and speaking to teachers and getting written reports, through to classroom observation visits and meetings aiming to close the 'school-home loop' (to create greater consistency between expectations and strategies used at home and at school).

Young people do not live as isolated individuals and their problems usually reflect difficulties in relation to someone, somewhere, or something. Our treatments should therefore reflect this.

## The first session

To give you a sense of what a first session in an OO-CAMHS service may look like, we have written out a more detailed example from a first session. These are only examples of the type of wording you may use. Each clinician will need to 'find their feet' with wording that makes sense for them and feels genuine. As clinicians we (at least in theory) should always reflect on what we do and say, to learn from our mistakes and successes so that we can keep improving our practice. The most important source of learning will be our patients' feedback. Finding a form of wording that works well is something that each clinician will have to discover for him or herself.

*Jade is a 15 year old girl who has lost weight over the past 6 months and has had no periods for the last 3 months. She attends the first session with her mother and father. The clinician is using the '© MyOutcomes 2012' online system on his laptop for patients to enter their ORS and SRS ratings.*

After introductions:

Clinician (C): *I'd like to explain a little about what will happen today. Firstly I like to do a quick family tree; this helps me understand who's in the family and who lives with who. After that and with your permission I would like to ask you to fill in a brief questionnaire that we use here called the Outcome Rating Scale. This will help give me a snapshot of where you see yourself as being at right now and what areas of your life you see as problematic or not. Once we have done this we'll spend some time talking about the reasons that you're here and what you hoped and how you imagined our service could help you. At the end of the session, again with your permission, I'll ask if you could fill in another short questionnaire, this time to get your feedback on today's meeting. All in all todays meeting will generally take somewhere between an hour and an hour and a half in total. Does that all sound OK to you? Great.*

After doing a basic genogram the clinician introduces the Outcome Rating Scale:

Clinician (C): *As I mentioned earlier, I would appreciate it very much if you could fill in this brief questionnaire called the Outcome Rating Scale. It gives us a 'ballpark' idea about where you see things are at, at the moment. If we carry on working together after today then I'm hoping you would be happy to continue doing this questionnaire at the start of each session. It doesn't take very long as there are only 4 questions, but it can help us keep an eye on how you see things are going; letting us know whether you feel things are improving from your point of view or not, so that if they're not improving we can discuss this and see if maybe we need to do something different. After all, the last thing I guess we want is for you to keep coming for appointments but nothing changes. Does that make sense to you?*

Mum (M) and dad (D) nod in affirmation, but Jade (J) keeps her head down looking at the floor.

C: *Jade, I would really appreciate if you wouldn't mind doing this questionnaire that I've got on the computer here. All you have to do is use the mouse to click on 4 different lines. If it's OK with you I'd also like to talk to you about your answers.*

C turns the laptop to face J with ORS showing.

C: *OK the first question asks you to think about how you feel in yourself. So thinking about the last few weeks where this side* [pointing to the far left of the first line as you look at the ORS] *is you've been feeling really unhappy or angry or frustrated and so on, and this side* [pointing to the far right of the first line as you look at the ORS] *you've been feeling really happy and good and relaxed and so on. Where would you rate yourself?*

J clicks the mouse at about 3 out of 10.

C: *So looking at that it seems you're rating how feel in yourself quite low, is that right?*

J: *Yes.*

C: *I'd really appreciate it if you could help me understand why you put your mark there.*

J: *I guess I'm not happy.*

J starts to cry, as she does so, so does M who reaches out to take her hand. C brings the box of tissues nearer to them.

C: *I can see how hard this is for you Jade and really admire your efforts so far. I wonder if you might be able to tell me more about this feeling unhappy, whether you have any ideas about what this might be about.*

J: [after some hesitation] *I just feel down all the time, I've got no energy, I know I should put weight on but I just can't do it and no one seems to understand so I feel so much pressure.* [Starts crying again]

C: *Thanks Jade, that's really helpful. So just to check out that I've got this right, the reason your mark is this low is because you feel unhappy, you have no energy, you know you're underweight but feel others don't understand how hard it is for you to change that and so you feel under a lot of pressure. Have I got that right?*

J nods her head.

C: *Thanks, that's really helpful. I did notice that you didn't put it right at the bottom so I'm also wondering whether there's a reason why its this far up, whether there are bits of you or times where you're not completely down?*

J: *The worst is at home, but I'm still seeing my friends and my school work is fine, so I do feel better when I'm at school or with my friends, although I know my mum and dad think I'm just kidding myself when I'm with them and trying to pretend I don't have a problem.*

J passes a 'if looks could kill' glance toward M.

C: *OK thanks, so from your point of view you feel somewhat better when you're at school or with your friends, but you think your parents think that you're not really feeling better at those times, just trying to bury or hide this eating problem you have, have I got that right?*

J nods her head.

The clinician then goes through the next 2 questions in the same manner asking for feedback on how Jade feels she's getting on in close relationships, meaning the immediate family she lives with and then how she feels she's getting on socially meaning at school and with friends. For close relationships Jade scores 1.4 out of 10, and explains that she knows her parents love her but there is a constant tension at home now, her mum cries a lot, her dad blames her for making her mum cry and so there are lots of arguments. It has been like that for a couple of months, but before that she wasn't someone who used to argue and tended to be someone who didn't like arguments or upset. For socially Jade scores 5.6 out of 10 explaining that its not what her parents think that she just buries her problems when she's with her friends, its more to do with getting away from all the tensions at home and 'having a laugh' with them makes her feel normal again. However, it has been getting more difficult as she has stopped being able to eat when they go to town and she now just gets a diet coke or something like that. Her friends have also started commenting about this and her weight loss, one friend even said 'you must be anorexic' in a jokey but probably serious way too.

C: *OK, last question now. This asks you to rate how feel overall, kind of putting everything that's going on in your life together onto one measure. One way to think about this question is to think about where you are in your life at the moment compared to where you would like to be where this side* [pointing to the far left of the last line as you look at the ORS] *is you're a million miles away from where you hoped to be in your life right now and this side* [pointing to the far right of the last line as you look at the ORS] *is your exactly where you wanted to be right now?*

J puts a 3.6 out of 10.

C: *Many thanks, that's really helpful. Is there anything you would like to add about the reasons you're here today that you haven't mentioned so far?* [J shrugs her shoulders] *OK. If you're happy with the ratings that you put then please click on the tick at the bottom of the page.*

A graph appears with session 1 rating on it for J that shows that J has scored 13.6 out of 40.

C: *So looking at the graph Jade, it seems that you have scored 13.6 out of a possible total of 40. That's quite a low score. This would suggest that you're not happy with your life right now and would really like things to change. Most people who are not looking for extra help tend to score above this red dotted line* [pointing at the clinical cut off line which is at 28] *and it looks like you're someway off from this at the moment. Does that make sense to you?* [J nods her head] *Thanks for your input Jade that's really helpful.*

C then asks J's parents to fill in the ORS: *I'd really appreciate if you could fill in the same questionnaire as Jade but this time it's about your perceptions of how you think*

*Jade is doing. Try and think about the reason you came here today as you fill this in, so that we can keep an eye on how you see things progressing from your point of view in future sessions. Remember you're rating how you perceived Jade to be doing, not how you're doing.*

Mum (M - who is still tearful) to dad (D): *you do it; I don't think I'm in any fit state to give my opinions.*

C turns the laptop to D: *I realize how upset you feel, but I think it's really important that you both give your opinions if you are able to. Could I suggest that you* [looking at M] *give your opinion to help your husband put marks that reflect your point of view too?*

As with J, D proceeds to fill each question in with C providing prompts for each question (e.g. "*Thinking about how you feel Jade is doing socially recently, which is mainly school and friendships, where would you rate Jade along this line where this side* [pointing to the far left as you look at the ORS] *is she's doing really badly, couldn't be worse and this side* [pointing to the far right as you look at the ORS] *is she's doing really well, couldn't be better?*"). M gave feedback on whether D's mark agrees with her perception or not. M suggests a couple of marks are moved down and so by the time they are happy with their scores they have put 2.7 out of 10 for intrapersonal, 3 for close relationships, 2.2 for socially and 2.5 for overall, giving a total score of 10.4 out of 40. As before C asks M and D what each mark means for them, which allows their ratings to connect to their reasons for attending.

About 17 minutes of the session has passed. Already C has a clear idea of each person's perception of the problem. The rating scale has been completed 'live' with feedback about the nature of the problems provided by the young person and her parents. The session then carries on as C gains further information and puts together a plan.

C: *As I mentioned at the start, just before you leave today, it would be really helpful for me if I could have some feedback from you about today's meeting. If it is all right with you, I do this using another brief questionnaire, which I will ask you to fill in on the laptop again. I realize it can be difficult to give honest feedback, particularly as we have only just met, but it is really helpful for all of us if you could be as honest as you can when answering each question. Research has shown that getting this feedback from the people who come to clinics like this can really help improve your chances of making progress. As professionals we are not always that good at knowing what particular approach, style or intervention is going to be most helpful, as everyone is different and we really need your help to help us to understand which bits work and which bits maybe don't work so well for you. Is that making some sort of sense to you?*

J, M and D nod in agreement. C turns the laptop towards J. The Session Rating Scale is showing on the laptop ready for J to fill in.

C: *Would it be OK to start with you Jade? Great. OK, there are four questions here and, like I said, I would really appreciate it if you could be as honest as you can when answering them. They are fairly self-explanatory really. The first one asks whether you felt I was listening to, understanding and respecting your opinions. The second one asks whether you felt we talked about what you hoped, wanted or felt we should have talked about and worked on in our meeting today. The third one asks how you feel about the approach we have decided to take, in other words your feelings about the treatment plan we put together today. Finally, the last question asks you how you felt about today's session overall. If you could just put a mark on the line using the mouse for each of these questions that would be really helpful.*

J then fills in the SRS and marks 9.5 for whether she felt listened to, 6 for how she felt about what we talked about, 6.5 for the approach/treatment plan and 8.2 for the session overall.

C: *Thanks Jade, I really appreciate that. It would be really helpful if you would be happy to explain the reasons behind your marks. For example, I would be really interested to understand how you felt about what we talked about in the meeting today.*

J [a little tearfully]: *Well I know we have to talk about all these things, but in truth, I don't really want to be here today. I find it really hard to talk about these things, my eating, all the arguments we're having and all that. I know we have to talk about it but I really don't want to.*

C: *Thanks Jade, that is really helpful. I could see how difficult all of this is for you and that was clear from the start of today's meeting. I actually think you have done incredibly well and shown a lot of courage coming here and being open and honest about things that are, understandably, very difficult for you. Would you be able to help me understand what you were thinking about when you put your mark for the approach that we agreed upon today?*

J: *I know I have to put on weight but I just don't think I can do this and I am not sure how I am going to cope with all this pressure I'm under.*

C: *Thanks once again Jade. I really appreciate your honesty and I gather how difficult all this feels for you. At this moment in time, as I mentioned earlier, my main focus is to see if we can get you back to good physical health and I guess, despite your very understandable concerns, I am hoping you might be able to give this plan a go and see how you get on. Is there anything else that you think I should or could be doing that would help you feel that what we are doing in these meetings would be more helpful or would work better for you?*

J: *I'm not sure. Maybe its my fault but I think you spent a lot of time talking to my parents and I don't think I got as much of a chance to say about things from my point of view.*

C: *I really appreciate that. That's really helpful. So it seems like you would have liked more time to explain your point of view and give your opinion and perhaps you're a little worried that this meeting was too much about how your parents see things and maybe even worried that I might as a result have kind of ended up on their side. Does that sound right to you?*

J nods.

C: *OK well we're a bit short of time to address that now, but I've made a note of this and next time we meet I'll make more of an effort to keep you involved in what we talk about and I will also meet with you one to one. Is that an OK next step for this?*

J nods.

C: *Thanks.*

C turns the laptop toward M and D.

C: *OK, could I get your feedback on today's meeting please. It is exactly the same questions as Jade has just answered but this time from your perspective about how you felt about today's meeting. As you can see, the four questions are to do with whether you felt listened to, understood and respected, whether you talked about what you hoped we would talk about or work on today, how you felt about my approach and, finally, how you felt about today's session overall. Again, I would really appreciate it if you could be as honest as possible. There is no such thing as bad feedback. All feedback is good and any tips you can give me on what works and does not work for you is much appreciated.*

D then uses the mouse to put marks on each question and asks his wife her opinion about each mark as they go along. They mark 9.6 for feeling listened to, understood and respected, 9.7 for talking about what they wanted to talk about, 9.8 for the approach, and 9.7 for the session overall.

C: *It looks, from your feedback, that overall you are quite happy with today's meeting and the plan that we made. Is that right?*

D: *Yes, it's been really helpful. We've been struggling to know what to do and it's good to get an expert's view.*

M: *For me, I've been constantly worried that I was doing the wrong thing. I've a much clearer idea now of what to do, although I am feeling guilty as to why I hadn't figured this out myself.*

C: *Feeling guilty is something that, as far as I can see, all of us who care about our children do. It's in the job description! I know, speaking as a parent myself, that, even though I'm a professional in this area, I seem to be constantly questioning what the right thing to do is with my children. Should I be more involved, should I be less involved, should I give more freedom, should I give more discipline, and so on. So your feeling guilty says to me that you're a loving parent, nothing more. Does that make sense?*

M [a little tearful] nods her head.

C: *I appreciate your taking the time to give me your feedback. Is there anything that occurred to you that you think you would have liked me to do differently or you would like me to do differently next time?*

M: *No, I don't think so.*

D: *Not for me, not at the moment.*

C: *OK, sometimes after people leave a meeting, something occurs to them, like they think 'Oh, I wish I had said that' or something occurs to them that, on reflection, they think 'actually, I think we needed more advice about this' or 'I'm not sure this is going to work', or whatever. If you do have any such thoughts occur to you, please make a note of them and, hopefully, we can talk about them when we next meet.*

C then makes an appointment for the next session, which M and D have indicated they would like to have take place the following week.

The above is a more detailed extract from a first session to give the reader a 'feel' of how using feedback rating scales is integrated into a clinical session. In real clinical practice each new patient and each new family is the beginning of a new therapeutic relationship. Whilst the basic ritual (such as using the ORS at the start and SRS at the end) will remain similar, the content of how these conversations get built up and made meaningful is likely to be unique. The tools that we use, hopefully, help us as clinicians develop our practice right from the first session in a manner that is as fully inclusive as possible of patients' and their families' opinions, values, cultures and practices. Different scenarios may bring up different combinations of who will be involved in filling in the ORS and SRS. Sometimes it will just be the young person who may have decided that they wish to be seen on their own. Sometimes it will be the young person and one parent, sometimes there will be two parents, but the clinician will decide they should fill one ORS between them (for example the clinician may want the parents to talk to each other and concentrate on their common ground). Sometimes each parent will fill a separate ORS about their child as they have different perspectives or an obvious disagreement about their child's problem. Sometimes siblings also attend and you may want their opinion about the referred young person or about themselves and how they feel they are doing, sometimes it can be another professional filling in the ORS such as a care worker from a children's home, a teacher, a social worker and so on.

## Scoring above the cut off for clinical significance

There are usually two reasons why a yp/p/c scores above the clinical cut off on the ORS at the first session. The most common reason is that the person who has put this score does not believe there is anything wrong or anything they need or want extra help with. For example a parent may rate their child low on the ORS as they are struggling with his/her behaviour, while the child rates things above the clinical cut-off as they are not particularly concerned or wishing to change their behaviour. Understanding these different perspectives can help with decisions about where to focus treatment efforts and who is motivated to change what. If both parent and their child score above the cut off, then it could be that another agency (such as school or social services) has recommended they go to CAMHS and they felt under pressure to do so despite not agreeing that this was necessary.

A second common reason for ratings being above the clinical cut-off at the first session is that the yp/p/c wants help with a very specific problem – one that does not impact the overall quality of life or functioning, such as a phobia or wanting to address concerns about how to prevent a particular past problem from recurring. Given the increased risk of deterioration for those who enter treatment above the clinical cut-off, clinicians are advised against entering into any extended or in-depth work and instead take a more a cautious approach. Discuss with the yp/p/c that they are scoring above the clinical cut-off and there is a risk (which gets higher the higher the initial ORS/CORS score is) that their score (and therefore sense of well-being) may deteriorate if it is decided to continue with treatment.

## Subsequent sessions

After the first session you will likely need to provide less and less guidance at subsequent sessions on filling in the ORS/SRS; but it is a good idea to risk 'overtraining' if you have any doubt about how well the yp/p/c understands or remembers how to do the ORC/CORS or SRS/CSRS.

Each session the ORS or CORS is given out at the beginning of the session to compare current ORS and CORS scores with previous ratings. Ratings are plotted on a graph so that the yp/p/c can see what is happening to their ratings. ***A change of 5 or more points on the ORS is considered significant***. If there is a change but of less than 5 points, this may still be meaningful, so it is always worthwhile discussing (however briefly) the graph of ORS scores once it has been plotted.

Clinician: *so looking at your scores they appear to have increased significantly. Does that sound right to you? [patient nods] In fact looking at the graph, you're rating an improvement that is substantially over the average expected improvement and puts you already close to the clinical cut off. That's pretty impressive. I'd really like to hear what you did to enable such a change to happen.*

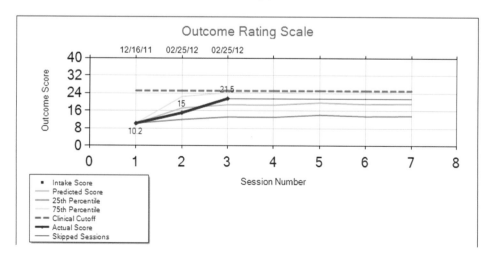

Or

Clinician: *Looking at the graph it seems there has only been a small change of a couple of marks. Usually that's not significant and means nothing much has changed since we last met. Does that sound right to you, or is that small change part of a small improvement.*

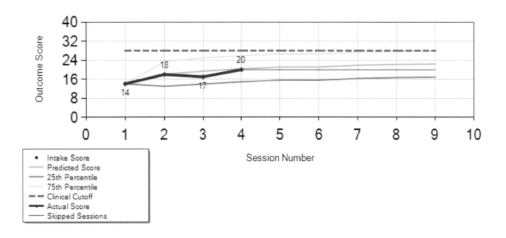

Or

Clinician: *Looking at the graph it seems there has only been a small change of a couple of marks with things maybe a little worse than last time. Usually a couple of points change is not significant and means nothing much has changed since we last met. Does that sound right to you? Are things more or less the same or have they got a little worse maybe?*

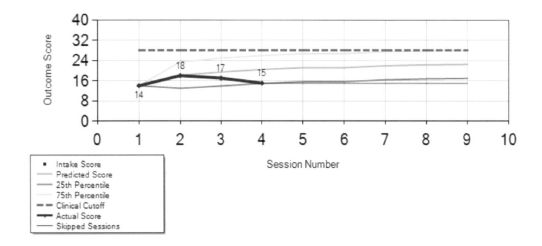

For much of the time you will be obtaining ratings from the young person and a parent or carer. Sometimes (e.g. with some behavioural problems) it will become apparent that it is mainly the parent/carer who wishes for change, in which case the therapeutic intervention may be mainly with them. If individual therapy is being offered to the young person, it is still important to try to capture the parent/carer's perceptions wherever possible by perhaps having a few minutes before the session at agreed intervals (for example every 2nd or 3rd session) when the parent/carer complete the ORS and then agree to review progress with the parent/ carer too after a set number of sessions (we would recommend about 5 or 6).

When using one of the computer software applications (such as '© MyOutcomes 2012'), you can also see how the yp/p/c score compares to a computer-generated 'expected treatment response' (ETR) for someone starting at the first session with any particular ORS score (see example below for someone scoring 9.3 on the first ORS). The ETR gives the clinician and yp/p/c the chance to compare their scores to the averaged trend of change, which has been calculated by pooling the results of over 300,000 episodes of treatment. On '© MyOutcomes 2012' The ETR shows up as lines representing the 25th percentile (according to the pooled data 25% score below this line), 50th percentile (50% in the dataset scored above and below), and 75th percentile  (25% in the dataset scored above this line). These ETR lines can be helpful in a number of ways, for example to highlight that someone is doing exceptionally, well, as well as at least half of those who come to treatment, or not doing as well as expected and so maybe need to think about what might need to change to improve the trajectory.

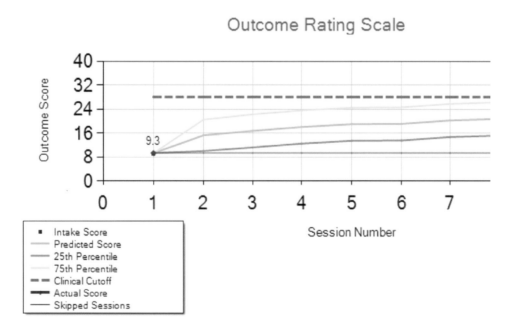

As sessions progress, scores will usually change. The graph will help maintain a visual record of these changes.

## Scores increase

When scores increase we can help patients see the importance of what they did to bring about changes.

To the young person: *This is encouraging, your score increased by about 5 marks from last time. How did you manage to accomplish this? What did you do different to make that happen? What have you learned about yourself through doing this?*

To their parent: *Your rating of Jo has gone up too. What do you think that's about? What have you and others in the family been doing differently, even if It's just a small change?*

## Scores stay the same or decrease

Clinician: *The scores haven't gone up again this time. What are you thoughts about why that is? What do you think we need to do differently to increase the chances of this line moving upward? What was it about what we have done so far that just didn't work for you, so I can change that?*

You might also find it helpful to go through each of the 4 items on the ORS individually for further ideas. For example:

Clinician: *So it looks like the interpersonal bit has stayed low. Is that right? It seems that the suggestion to work on noticing and re-enforcing positives hasn't quite worked as we hoped, or perhaps it's just too early to tell. Could we talk about that to help me understand what happened with this suggestion and whether we need to troubleshoot on it or perhaps find a different approach?*

## Scores stay low by session 5

When ORS ratings stay low by session 5, then its time to review the treatment more thoroughly.

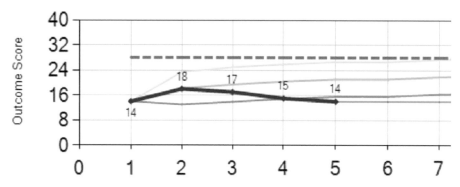

Clinician: *It looks like you're still rating things about the same as when we started. Is that right? I think it's time for us to spend a bit of time thinking about this. Unfortunately, the research evidence suggests that if you are going to benefit from*

*the work we've been doing together we should have seen some positive changes by now. Although that's not true for everyone, I guess I'm a bit concerned that maybe we need to have a serious think about what we're doing and try and make some changes. As I mentioned when we first met, in our service we like to review what we're doing if there's been no improvement by session 5. It could be that we should try a different approach or maybe through no fault of yourselves or for that matter me, we are just not the right fit and maybe you might make more progress with someone else. Would it be OK to talk a bit more about this?*

A number of options could be 'put on the table' to talk about including: changing the treatment in someway, such as introducing another modality (e.g. seeing the young person for individual sessions if family meetings have been done so far or visa versa), introducing a different model (such as more insight orientated psychodynamic, more cognitive behavioural, more solution focussed etc.), adding another clinician (for example working with a co-therapist), changing clinician, referral for another service (such as a group intervention, a different agency), or agreeing to carry on with the same intervention but agree how long you would carry this on for before reviewing options to change. This is also a good time to take the case for supervision or multi-disciplinary team discussion.

### Low SRS/CSRS scores

Any low SRS scores should be addressed (and then acted on) at each session. If they remain low check the reasons for this and whether it might be better for the yp/p/c to try a different clinician. Remember we should not view this as a failure for either the clinician or young person or their family. It's probably just a matter of not being the right 'fit'. Like personal relationships, professional relationships often come down to unquantifiable aspects like a lack of 'personal chemistry'.

## Preparing for discharge

One of the big changes that services that have adopted PCOMS have found is that the average number of sessions that patients are seen by the service goes down and with it the numbers of people who are 'stuck in the system' being seen for many months or years. This long term involvement can happen even though the young person is not improving or because they are believed to have a 'chronic condition' requiring on-going input or even because they have a good therapeutic relationship and the clinician struggles with 'saying goodbye'. Research has shown that, not only the longer a treatment goes on without evidence of positive change the greater the likelihood that the episode of treatment will not be successful, but also that less and less change happens the longer a treatment goes on (i.e. most of the change for most people happens in the earlier sessions). Of course such findings do not mean that there is no place for long term work or that patients who don't show evidence of early change will never change later in the course of a treatment episode, just that it is less likely to happen. A significant part of clinician's caseload and a significant factor behind clinician burn-out are the 'heart-sink' patients, stuck in the system absorbing resources but without significant change. An outcome focus can help change this. Keeping a focus on outcomes can make a big difference to successfully discharging patients earlier.

## Discharging after one session

Many families will be seen for one session only and then discharged. The first session (the 'Choice' appointment in the CAPA model) is an opportunity to understand the presenting problem, areas that the yp/p/c are rating low, but also the areas they are rating as being good and thus could have positive resources. It is also an opportunity to explore what CAMHS may or indeed may not be able to help with.

There are a number of reasons why you may choose to discharge the young person after the first session. These include: the referral being made at a moment of crisis which has since passed and the family are no longer seeking further help, the type of help needed is better provided by another service (e.g. through education), the problems experienced by the yp/p/c are not of a severe enough degree to warrant CAMHS intervention that may thus medicalise/problematize ordinary experience.

The assessment of severity is aided by the ORS ratings (see pages 49 – 54 and **'The Outcome and Session Rating Scales'**, pages 26 - 34). When the young person or their carer rates above the clinical cut off this should be discussed with them and explained that further treatment could result in a reduction of these scores with the accompanying possibility that the sense of well-being deteriorates too.

## Discharging too early

Discharging too late is a much more common problem than discharging too early. However, the possibility of discharging before any gains have stabilised should also be kept in mind. When scores have significantly increase and/or reached over the clinical cut off, then give it a session or more to see if the gains are maintained before discussing discharge. Improvements can be viewed as opportunities to discuss what the yp/p/c did that helped make a difference and how they might keep this improvement going. Prior to the conversation about discharge consider increasing the time between appointments.

## Discharging too late

A more common issue is that patients are kept with the service longer than they need to be. We would recommend conversations that include a discussion about discharge start as soon as there is evidence that the young person (according to the primary rating, which could be the young person and/or their parent or carer) has reached above clinical cut-off or when scores have plateaued for at least 2 or 3 sessions after initial improvement. This doesn't mean the young person must be discharged from the service at this point, it just means that a conversation about discharge can take place.

In that conversation the progress on the ORS graph can be looked at and be integrated into the conversation. When people have reached the likely benefit they are going to get from coming to a service, but carry on being seen, there is a danger that their well being will fall back over time. In addition we want people to leave our services as soon as possible. However good it makes us as clinicians feel, we hope that our patients leave impressed by their resources and capacity for healing, not ours. We should therefore keep a mind-set prepared to act by talking about the subject of discharge as soon as we see signs that the yp/p/c has stabilised any improvement. It also then conveys our confidence that they are ready to manage without us.

## Discharge conversations

A conversation about discharge can start by simply laying out a few choices.

Clinician: *Looking at your ORS graph it seems that you have rated above the clinical cut off for 2 sessions now after gradually improving for the 3 sessions before then. Does that sound right and make sense? This is the time we usually talk about discharge. What you've done since coming here has been very impressive and I think you're ready to build on this progress outside of here now. I generally recommend three main options at this stage. First if you, like me, think you're ready then we could discharge Hannah today. Second, if you don't quite feel ready yet then we could arrange another appointment but space it out much longer than usual, say in 3 months time and if when we meet then your ratings are still good, we can discharge at that meeting. If not of course we can discuss what we should do about it instead. The third option is that I keep the notes open for 3 months, but we don't make another appointment. If you don't contact us by the end of those 3 months, I'll assume all is still well and we will discharge Hannah then. Of course these are just my suggestions. It's important that we do what you think is right, so if you felt you wanted a bit longer before we tried one of these 3 options, that's absolutely fine although I think it would be helpful if we could decide how long or how many sessions more we should have before you think you might be ready to revisit those 3 options.*

Discharge is an opportunity to review what has made a difference and help the yp/p/c think about their contribution to the improvement. Some useful questions to help this process include:

*If I were to see another family who came to see me and explained a set of problems very similar to the ones you explained to me when we first started, what advice would you give them?*

*What was it about what you did that made the difference?*

*What did you discover about yourself since coming here?*

*If you were to have a box, which I'll call your mental health first aid box, what personal things could you put in there to remind you of what made a difference in the last few months that might help you through the next set of obstacle you will face?*

## When no improvement occurs after 2 or more unsuccessful treatment episodes

We are not miracle workers and whilst we should always extend our best efforts to help those who come to our services, sometimes despite these best efforts and despite remaining patient centred and outcome informed, several treatment episodes later there is still no change.

Whilst we should always strive to maintain a capacity to see the world through our patient's eyes and see the potential good in everyone, we must also remain realistic. We won't hit it off with everyone and some people won't hit it off with anyone in our service. Furthermore, safeguarding issues that we have to address may rear its head and this may put our service in a family's 'bad books'. At other times the difference in perspective between a young person and their parents may be insurmountable pushing the clinicians into a perception that they must take sides however hard that clinician has strived not to. Sometimes we need to take sides as the young person, though not formally being abused is nonetheless being treated unfairly, or vice versa the young person is behaving in an unreasonable manner that is difficult to ignore. In other words there will always be some people who we will not, as a service be able to help. Keeping them engaged with services that are not of benefit and have little likelihood of being any benefit wastes resources whilst helping no one.

We need to learn to be brave enough to have discussions about discharge with such yp/p/c. This needn't be blaming or persecutory. Instead we can be honest and reflective and help them think about alternatives:

Clinician: *Well looking at the graph it seems that we haven't made any progress and this is the 6th meeting. I would have expected some changes by now if we were going to be successful in helping you. I realise you have seen a couple of other people before meeting with me and a similar thing happened. I'm thinking therefore that we are probably the wrong service or this is the wrong time. This is not a criticism of you. Everybody is different and people find that things that help them are different, or sometimes it's just the wrong time to make changes in their lives. I would like to talk to you therefore about whether we should take a break, perhaps you need time to mull things over and think about some of the suggestions I and (names of the other two clinicians) made and whether any of them could be something worth revisiting in the future or whether we should be making a referral to another service.*

Remember, this does not mean that there is never a place for long term work with little evidence of improvement. It just means we should always think carefully with yp/p/c about this. Sometimes for example such work may help prevent a deterioration or be part of a deliberate risk management strategy (for example, you may not want to discharge someone who is actively suicidal even if it has proved difficult to produce change. Keeping them engaged with services may prove life saving).

# OO Team Meetings

**This section will cover:**

- The importance of building good team relationships through noticing and re-enforcing the positive attributes of clinicians.

- Building capacity for team reflection.

- Understanding the role of leadership.

A good team ethos and sense of identity built around supportive relationships are an integral part of developing and maintaining good therapeutic practice in CAMHS. Teams are usually the drivers of change when service transformation is the desired outcome. Individuals can make important differences, but, especially if they sit lower in the power hierarchy, changing practice at the individual clinician level, without having a supportive set of professional relationships, rarely succeeds. Team dynamics will have an important role to play. A flattening of the power hierarchy is a goal of OO sessions and mirroring this in team relationships is a goal of a well functioning OO team. This does not mean that hierarchies will disappear and that the impact on overall team dynamics can ever be evened out in equal proportions amongst the team members. It does mean that this should be at least thought about and struggled with.

## Useful questions for a team ponder include

Who has authority and why?

Who holds responsibility and for what?

Who has expertise and in what?

Who holds or understands the 'expert by experience' perspective?

How do inter-professional relationships work in this team?

How can we improve our professional relationships and trust in each other?

How can we best help each other?

What is the power hierarchy?

How can voices from lower down this hierarchy be included?

How can we avoid 'tokenism'?

How can we contain the fact that there will be different opinions?

How can we privilege debate over consensus?

How are questions of race, culture, and gender dealt with in our team?

How do we get beyond diagnostic thinking?

How can we keep an element of outcome focus in our clinical discussion?

How much notice do we really take of the therapeutic relationship?

Do we prefer a more formal or informal format?

What are we good at and what do we need to work on?

How are we going to celebrate what we're good at?

The above is just a short list of possible questions, some analytic, others active and change orientated. There are endless variations to these questions and we would encourage each team to discover their own voice and identity by working on questions and areas of change that they feel is of most relevance to them. These questions can be formulated in team meetings and discussed at team building away days or workshops.

Many teams are understandably sick of team building, service redesign and outside agency consultation. There has been a growing managerial culture imported into the health service using industry-based models. This is not what we are advocating. Building good relationships is much more fluid and nuanced and not easily reducible to a flow diagram or a set of 'how to' steps prescribed by a manual. We think good relationships are created and discovered in the course of on-going interactions. We are merely suggesting teams create formats that can facilitate on-going exchange of thoughts and opinions (interactions) about issues, questions, and aspects they would like to change.

## Leadership

Teams that are functional will have a sense of leadership. Although the aim is to create a democratic and inclusive culture, someone or a number of people identified formally or informally as in leadership positions forge a sense of direction, goals, and identity.

Those in leadership positions will have a disproportionate impact on the culture of the team and have a particular responsibility to contribute toward creating a positive, outcome orientated, and inclusive culture.

## Some ideas for OO-team meetings

Bring cases for clinical discussion. Include discussions about the ORS and SRS scores. Focus clinical discussions on ideas for change/doing something different when there is a lack of improvement.

Make sure there is careful co-ordination of cases discussed at team meetings (which act as peer supervision) and those discussed in one to one supervision. Supervision duplication can cause similar problems to treatment duplication leading to clinicians possibly getting conflicting advice.

Bring cases back for discussion particularly when they have been seen for 5 sessions with no improvement. Consider setting up a '5 session clinic' either as a supervision group or as a live consultation with a reflecting team.

Move away from diagnostic questions that may lead to iatrogenic dependency. We are aware that this may lead at times away from reliance on NICE guidelines. NICE guidelines it should be remembered are guidelines. They provide recommendations on processes that will hopefully lead to better outcomes, however, they do not include recommendations on how to rate outcomes. If we can demonstrate that the patient, as a result of an intervention reports positive change, this is more important than whether we adhered to a particular process guideline. In addition, as discussed previously, there is little evidence to support that diagnosis helps in decisions about treatment in a way that will differentially affect outcome. Diagnostic focussed interventions (as opposed to change focussed ones) also risk embedding narratives of chronicity and with it expectations of the service having long-term involvement in on-going treatment, which is often (but not always) unnecessary.

Bring whole team data to meetings from time to time (for example once a month). This is often full of good news and shows that patients are reporting positive changes. This is one way of doing something we are generally not very good at doing, which is noticing and celebrating our successes.

Work toward a flattening of professional hierarchies. Good leadership should encourage a culture of inclusion and a place for diverse opinions to be expressed.

Work hard to avoid professional 'silos' developing. Try to create a Multi-Disciplinary Team (MDT) that is a MDT, not people working in isolation, each doing their own thing. In particular psychology and psychiatry often get split. Although sometimes it may need to be accepted that differences are just too large to bridge, on the whole differing opinions help create a richness that can be valuable.

Develop confidence in standing up for patient's rights. Clinical practice should be focussed on improving outcomes. Teams will accumulate data that will show whether that is being achieved. Sometimes searching questions will need asking, particularly if data is showing more patients are in long term care compared to other teams, or there is higher DNA rate, or there are poorer outcomes.

Reflect on what you're good at and what you're not. Use outcome data to help. Think about what might be done differently in areas the team needs to improve on (for example you may try a parenting group if behaviour problems don't seem to be improving in individual appointments).

Avoid the idea of 'treatment silos' too. Clinician skills come from training in different perspectives, personal interests and interpersonal skills in therapy. The task of a team is to create patient orientated reflective practice, rather than make ideological commitments to one brand or a narrow concept of treatment.

Have a healthy respect for clinician autonomy.

Try new initiatives and be creative (as long as you are rating whether your project is resulting in improved outcomes). Group work can be rewarding and efficient and often results in involving several members of the team facilitating the group together. Joint work like this helps build relationships.

Service users (both young people and their parents or carers) opinions and ideas are often of great benefit to a team. Getting input that represents the diversity of the community served is important. Solicit feedback from individual sessions, surveys or focus groups. Invite users to meetings and to be members of a steering group.

# OO Supervision and Management

**This section will cover:**

- Linking supervision to the CORE principles.

- Using data from the ORS and SRS to integrate patient feedback into supervision.

- Common problems that may emerge that decreases clinician effectiveness.

- Identifying and responding to possible concerns.

- Creating a management culture that supports clinicians in their efforts to become Outcome Orientated.

Where traditionally supervisors are guided by a particular treatment model or theoretical orientation, OO supervision is guided by both theoretical/treatment model AND routine outcome and alliance feedback from patients. OO supervision links the feedback yp/p/c are giving about their progress and therapeutic relationship with an understanding of the treatment process and a capacity to remain flexible with the direction being led by the feedback the yp/p/c are giving about the treatment they are receiving. Great OO supervisors are able to combine their theoretical therapeutic knowledge with the CORE principles, remaining aware of the importance of the system around the young person (for example knowing when 'consultation' with other agencies is needed) and building a positive team ethos as well as maintaining an awareness of outcome and alliance issues in individual case supervision.

OO management supports the whole system by championing the development of an OO culture and remaining aware of the 3 most important factors associated with successful implementation projects: Clinician buy in, data management, and data integrity (see **'Putting the OO into the CAMHS Team'** pages 40 – 48).

# Supervision

The supervisor will act as a role model focussing on building good relationships with clinicians and noticing their positives and strengths (although not ignoring any problems). The OO-CAMHS model will function more effectively within teams if the key concepts of the approach are incorporated into regular clinician meetings and conversations, such as clinical supervision sessions. Having a focus on outcome management will improve the consistency and integrity of the model for the whole team. It's important that supervisors have a good understanding of the OO-CAMHS approach and understand how to interpret patient data so as to help the supervisee relate clinical session information to outcome and session rating scores.

Good supervision is integral to every CAMHS clinician's work and incorporating the OO-CAMHS components effectively into this supervision will increase the likelihood that clinicians will 'buy in' to the model, better understand how the outcome data is managed, and improve the integrity of how yp/p/c's desired outcomes are incorporated into therapeutic sessions.

## Incorporating the CORE principles

A part of the supervisory process will be to reinforce the four guiding principles that underpin the OO-CAMHS approach in order to promote a culture of recovery from the outset. The aim is to produce the best outcomes by ensuring that the most effective therapeutic process and relationship is established, through:

- *Consultation:*

Maintain an awareness of extra-therapeutic factors. Remember, extra-therapeutic factors account for 40-87% of the variance of outcome in CAMHS.

Involve the yp/p/c in reviewing environmental factors that may impact on likelihood of success in treatment.

Consider who is best placed to have a meaningful relationship with the yp/p/c.

Suggest keeping the process simple so that not too many professionals are unnecessarily involved - trying to avoid more than one agency working on any one problem at any one time. Advise that duplication of therapeutic input is usually confusing for the patient despite the best intentions of professionals and can result in complex cases being created. Reducing to the minimum the number of professionals involved is often more empowering than increasing them. Sometimes, it is better to delay becoming involved or indeed decline becoming involved until the other agency/ worker has finished their therapeutic input.

Decide whether the circumstances are favourable for treatment. Consider whether there are there stable contact arrangements in place, support from the parent, involvement from the courts etc., which may disrupt the stability, predictability, confidentiality, or safety of the therapeutic intervention.

Ensure, where necessary, that multi-agency professional meetings are established and take place to avoid duplication. Remember that joint work needs careful co-ordination, particularly when one agency or more are already involved, social services are involved, or the child is in care.

Avoid long term treatment with no discernable or measurable benefit. Consider wider systemic and extra-therapeutic factors that may interfere with or inhibit the usefulness of any treatment on offer.

- *Outcome*:

Monitoring outcomes of yp/p/c session-by-session using ORS/SRS (either by using graphs provided by online feedback systems or by charting manually on paper) with regular feedback to the yp/p/c about how they are progressing, not only improves outcomes but also helps to shape the direction of the treatment. It provides an early alert to poor treatment response and helps the clinician to focus on whether what they and their patient are doing together is making a meaningful difference from the patients' point of view. Feedback on the subjective experience of change and therapeutic alliance from the yp/p/c can act like an early warning system to prevent drop-outs and negative outcomes. If no change is observed by session 5 it is important to discuss this in supervision (whether individual or multi-disciplinary team) as well as with yp/p/c.

The supervisor should have access to their supervisee's outcome data and examine this for:

1. Evidence that the ORS and SRS are being done,
2. To spot cases that are not improving, particularly if they have had 5 sessions or more.
3. The supervisee's overall outcome data in relation to others in the team.

In particular the supervisor should discuss cases not improving. Patterns of ORS scores most frequently associated with risk for dropout or negative outcome are: outcome score above the clinical cut off (i.e., not showing much distress) at intake; high and flat outcome score from session to session, indicating that the patient may have achieved the maximum benefit of service; outcome scores that remains unchanged or that decreases over time; and fluctuating outcome scores.

ORS scores that decrease suddenly and dramatically often present a different concern than a steady decline would create. Whereas a steady decline may point to problems with the quality/usefulness of the treatment episode, a sudden and sharp drop in ORS scores often results from unexpected, external events that are either unrelated or tangential to treatment.

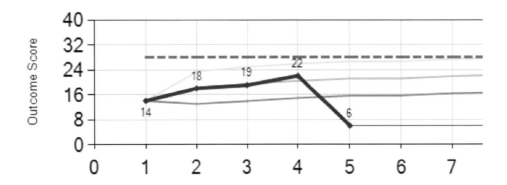

ORS scores can also fluctuate in a see-saw fashion for several reasons including: the patient not carefully following or understanding the directions when completing the ORS form; normal variation in nonclinical levels of functioning, typical of everyday life; or ineffective treatment. Each of these circumstances carries some risk of patients feeling disempowered over time and/or dropping out of services. See-saw scores are often a result of patients completing the form based on how they feel at the time, rather than since the last meeting. For patients who start above the clinical cut-off, or who have met and exceeded the benchmark of predicted change, some variation in ORS scores is typical and reflects normal variation in day-to-day (or week-to-week) functioning.

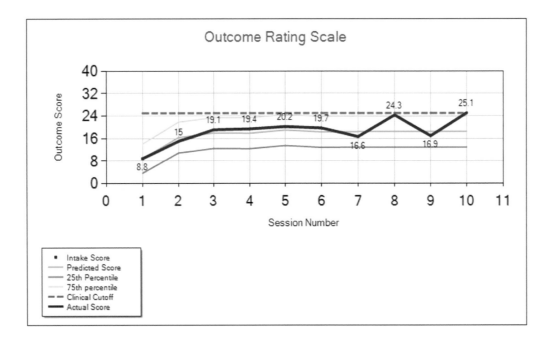

- *Relationship*:

People are often reluctant to highlight problems or issues they have if simply invited to comment on how they experience the session. Using the SRS session by session from the outset will establish a ritual in treatment sessions that will formally invite feedback. Refer to the SRS scores and check that the clinician is discussing the scores and acting on any concerns that arise in the feedback. Persistent problematic alliance is associated with a high risk for dropout or negative outcome. Where cases are not improving look at the SRS and discuss the therapeutic relationship. Emphasise that the score the yp/p/c gives on the alliance measure is not as important as having the conversation with them about what can be done differently to improve the treatment from their perspective.

- *Ethics of care*:

Building a positive team culture that is supportive to teams trying to put patient engagement and voice at the heart of their approach is crucial to the successful implementation of OO-CAMHS. Like patients, clinicians work better when they feel valued, listened to, and taken seriously. Encourage taking stuck cases to peer group supervision for discussion. This can encourage different perspectives, and generate new ideas. Getting everyone in the team talking about outcomes and CORE principles, may also be helpful in addressing some clinician's scepticism and concern about the model. It is reassuring to hear about other clinicians' experiences of the benefits of using formal feedback in their work and to celebrate team accomplishments. Be an active member of the team. Support the team in a positive way and use the ideas discussed in **'OO-Team Meetings'** (pages 71 – 74) above.

## Possible clinician related problems causing lack of progress in treatment

Below is a list of issues that may emerge and the supervisor may wish to check with their supervisees:

*Are outcome and alliance measurement tools being completed at each session?*

*Is yp/p/c feedback about well-being and about the therapeutic alliance being used? If so, how?*

*Do outcome scores indicate that the yp/p/c is making progress?*

*Do scores on alliance measures reflect positive relationships?*

*If no progress is evident or alliance measures indicate possible concerns, is the clinician addressing this with the yp/p/c?*

*What is the plan to address lack of progress or alliance issues?*

*Has the clinician explored what the yp/p/c wants from treatment?*

*Has the yp/p/c stated a goal for treatment?*

*Has the clinician asked the yp/p/c what his or her ideas are about how change happens?*

*Has the clinician asked the yp/p/c about his or her preferences regarding the therapy relationship (i.e., gender preferences, cultural awareness, specialized approaches, etc.)?*

*Has the clinician asked the yp/p/c about his or her expectations regarding the clinician's role?*

*Is the clinician discussing outcome and alliance scores and the meaning the yp/p/c puts to those scores with them?*

*Is the yp/p/c languishing in therapy with no evident impact?*

*Is it time to discuss discharge?*


More serious potential problems that may need more active intervention and suggestions by the supervisor include:

*Clinician takes an overly diagnostic, distancing, or patient-blaming perspective.*

*Clinician is unable to describe yp/p/c preferences or goals for treatment.*

*Clinician is vague about how outcome and alliance measures are used in practice.*

*Clinician's no-show or dropout rates are high.*

*Clinician continues to see yp/p/c for long periods despite an absence of measurable progress.*

*Alliance scores consistently reflect problems with therapeutic relationships.*

*Clinician sees the formal use of outcome and alliance measures as an administrative rather than a clinical task.*

*Clinician outcomes are consistently lower than others with no accompanying clinical reason of why that should be the case (such as specialising in more complex cases).*


New directions when there is no progress in treatment after 5 sessions can include:

*Different activities, methods, or models of treatment.*

*Inviting others to sessions (such as a parent who hasn't thus far been involved).*

*Examining role of extended family.*

*Examining extra-therapeutic factors such as broader social and financial well-being.*

*Examining other community resources.*

*Changing the frequency of meetings.*

Change in treatment clinician make up can include:

*Use of reflecting team.*

*Use of consultant (psychologist, psychiatrist, team leader, etc.) to join for one off session with yp/p/c.*

*Use of consultant or second clinician to join as co-therapist.*

*Use of consultant or second clinician to work in parallel (for example one seeing young person, the other seeing a parent), providing there are regular opportunities to discuss and keep the work co-ordinated.*

*Referral to an alternative clinician in the team.*

*Referral to a different team within the service.*

*Referral to a new agency.*

*Normalisation and discharge.*

## An example supervision session

Below is an example script of how a supervision session can become outcome orientated:

**Supervisor:** *Hi Jordan, as we've already discussed, we're going to shift our supervision sessions from now on to incorporate the OO-CAMHS model so I guess it'll take both of us a while to get used to that. I hope this is still OK and I'm wondering how you have been getting on with using, the ORS and SRS, at the start and end of each session?*

**Jordan:** *Yes it would be good to go over the new ideas. I've been using the rating scales with my patients for a little while now, so I think I'm beginning to get into the routine of using them. I must admit that there have been times when I have forgot to use one of the measures at the start or end of a session, but I soon realise once I logged onto the computer programme to put the ratings in.*

**Supervisor:** *I guess that will become less of an issue once you have been using it for longer. The more you use it, the easier it becomes until eventually its just a routine part of your therapy 'ritual'. I'm glad you've been honest about this, because I think this is such a common problem at the start. It takes time just to become a part of your* *normal and routine therapeutic mind-set, but it is important to get used to doing it. I've been looking at your data set and I wonder if we could bring up the data about this patient that I mentioned I wouldn't mind talking about? Did you bring their notes?*

**Jordan:** *Yes and I've got the computer programme loaded up here with their graphs. This is from a boy called 'Joshua', a 14 year old boy who has seen me for five sessions now, here are his scores for the Outcome Rating Scale:*

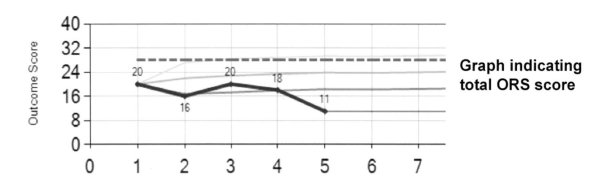

**Graph indicating total ORS score**

**Jordan:** *As you can see from the graph, Joshua has repeatedly scored quite low and his most recent scores suggest that he's getting worse. He reinforced the scores by telling me that he feels as if things have been getting worse for him, I'm worried about what to do. Should I change what I am doing with him or keep continuing my therapy and hope that things get better?*

**Supervisor:** *OK, lets see if we can understand what factors could account for the Joshua's rating of their current outcome. Remember how extra-therapeutic factors and therapeutic relationship can influence outcomes to a much greater extent than the choice of therapeutic approach? It could be that it is not your therapy but something else that is affecting Joshua's scores, perhaps we should look into this first.*

**Jordan:** *OK, that makes some sense. I must admit that I do feel that I'm using an evidenced-based approach and I have found that this therapy has worked for other people with similar issues. I'm still not sure what to do next but I'll show you Joshua's scores in detail for each week.*

**Supervisor:** *Right, thanks for getting that information ready. I can see that in the first week Joshua is rating himself and school/work at 4, his family score is 7, and overall at 5. Interesting that his family score is highest...did you explore this?*

**Jordan:** *Yes, Joshua felt that his mum was a good support and he could go to her for help when he was feeling sad and low. He also felt that he could go to his dad, but often his dad has to work away from home, for weeks at a time, so he wasn't always able to get his help. I did ask Joshua how his scores could be higher in this area and he felt that two things could really help. One, his dad could be around more often, not going* *away for long periods, and two his younger brother could stop annoying him so much.*

**Supervisor:** *How about the other scores? Did you find out anything there?*

**Jordan:** *Regarding the score for his personal well-being, he stated that he had felt this way for a while now and he wasn't sure what could improve things. In terms of school, he said he hated everything and everyone at school and didn't really like going. He only goes to keep mum and dad off his back about it. He couldn't think of anything to improve things here either. Although in my last session with him he mentioned that someone at school had been nasty to him again. He refused to say anything more about this.*

**Supervisor:** *It sounds like there might be some issues there. I'm wondering what scores have dropped in his last session, was it those relating to his school or something else.*

**Jordan:** *let me see...in session 4 his scores were about the same in all areas, however in session 5 his score for his personal well-being was still 4, but his 'Interpersonal' score had dropped to 3 and his 'Socially' score was at 1, with an overall score of 3. I asked him how come his scores about his family had gone down and he said that his dad had gone away again. He didn't elaborate, but I wonder if things are not good between his mum and dad. When I asked about school he just shrugged his shoulders. I'm worried about this and so is his mother, who has contacted the school but she was reassured by the class teacher that nothing untoward had been observed. Joshua is mixed race and you know his school has mainly white kids, so I don't know if that's an issue.*

**Supervisor:** *Did you ask about whether he's experiencing racism or being picked on because of is background, or have you asked about how he and his mother see themselves?*

**Jordan:** *Well it went through my mind, but I didn't ask about this no..............*

As can be seen, the clinical supervision session can still follow within the parameters of the usual conversation had between supervisor and supervisee, with the OO-CAMHS components interspersed within to guide the discussion towards areas of concern and possible solutions. Although this example focused on the ORS, given at the start of each clinical session, it may also be useful to bring in the data about the therapeutic relationship gathered from the SRS, given at the end of each session. Supervision can utilise one or more components of the OO-CAMHS model in order to help formulate the patient's issues and better understand what may be going on and where to introduce ideas that may lead to new ways forward emerging.

As in the example above, with the supervisee getting to grips with remembering to use the measures with the yp/p/c in the sessions, the more that OO-CAMHS is incorporated into the dynamics of the functioning of the team, such as supervision and team meetings, the more efficient clinicians will be at utilising the ideas and sharing the 'common language' of this approach with each other.

## Management

The role of a manager is to support the implementation of the OO-CAMHS model in the service. In helping support the implementation in a manner that results in service transformation, less is more. By this we mean that managers need to support the implementation, allow time for staff training, approach commissioners etc., but avoid micro-management and getting too involved in the data set.

Remember the key factors associated with successful service transformation projects are:

- **Clinician buy in.** The more clinicians are willing to adopt the approach the greater the likelihood of success.
- **Data management**. Detailed outcome data on a clinician by clinician basis will become available. Clinicians need to know that this will not be used or accessed by managers to make decisions about hiring and firing. Proper explicit and transparent agreements that protect clinician integrity are needed.
- **Data integrity.** The quicker a full dataset with outcome data on the ORS and SRS for all patients is achieved, the greater the likelihood that the service transformation aims will be realised. Management can support this as a priority.

These three factors are of course related. The better the clinician buy-in, the easier data integrity will be to achieve, and the clearer the data management procedures are, the easier it will be to get clinician buy in and so on.

Managers can support the importance of good and non-persecutory data management, put data reporting procedures in place and make explicit recommendations, policies, and practice guidelines.

These policies should focus on the implementation of robust OO-CAMHS protocols and an understanding of how data will be collected and what reports will be made and to whom.

Management and processing of patients, clinician supervision, clinician outcome data and building a team ethos should be left in the hand of team leaders and supervisors. Overall managers of the service can provide and support guidelines on the implementation of OO-CAMHS. This will include decisions about what method of data collection to use (paper or computer based), what data to collect and review (on a team by team basis), what training to support is needed, and so on.

## Data collection

Data collection by paper versions of ORS and SRS, has the advantage of being free for individual users to download and they can go straight into the notes and thus be easily available for review by the clinician. The disadvantages include needing another method to collate the outcome data, more time consuming to check on data integrity (i.e. that clinicians are using the ORS/SRS for all patients in nearly all sessions), measuring and scoring by hand means it's a little more time consuming, and there is less information available (such as comparison with expected treatment response, automatic calculation of team or clinician overall data etc.). Data collection will therefore need to be done manually using an Excel spread-sheet (See **'Developing a Database'** pages 87 – 90).

Data collection through computer aided systems like '© MyOutcomes 2012' have the advantage of ease of use, calculations are done automatically, graphs are produced automatically and data is generated as you go along. Clinician and whole team data quickly becomes available as does a comprehensive data base of outcomes. Children and young people seem to like using the system and it gives an impression of a 'modern' and professional service. The main disadvantage is that this system costs, with an annual subscription fee payable per clinician. The amount is relatively small (about £85 per clinician per year at the time of writing this in March 2012).

Other problems with the system include that its language is orientated to an American audience, as is its date system, and the lack of ability to include other useful data on the system (like DNAs).

Decisions on what other outcome rating scales to use in addition to the ORS will need to be taken in consultation with commissioners. Using the ORS is compatible with using other non-session-by-session measures recommended by CORC including the Strengths and Difficulties Questionnaire (SDQ) and CHI Experience of Service Questionnaire (CHI-ESQ). We would like to hope that in the future the SDQ will be dispensed with as thus far it has not proved a reliable source of outcome information due to low levels of second ratings return and we do not believe it adds any extra useful data that cannot be taken from the more robust and reliable database derived from the ORS ratings. We would recommend against using as a routine any other session-by-session rating scales concurrently with the ORS, as this adds unnecessary paperwork and an extra burden of time. Clinicians may also use other scales (in addition to the ORS/SRS) that are related to their assessment or treatment modality and depending on their personal preferences.

Other data that could be considered as part of the dataset includes: DNA and cancellation rate, Length in treatment, average number of sessions of treatment, referral rate to tier 4 services (such as in-patient units) and so on (see **'Key Performance Indicators'** pages 116 - 120).

Finally outcome data could be linked to a variety of other data of potential interest, for example the data could be analysed by age, by diagnostic clusters, by ethnicity, by type of intervention (for example individual or family), etc. This can help in identifying areas of good practice and areas that could benefit from further development.

## Data management

Clear policies on data management and data collection should be drawn up. We would recommend that when starting an OO-CAMHS service transformation project, the policy should be that the ORS/CORS and SRS/CSRS is expected to be used for all patients, however, the database of outcomes will be built up by using the data for all new patents seen by the service after the start date for the project. All existing cases can have the paper versions administered, but would not be included as part of the database being built up. This allows for a culture of outcomes to be incorporated into the service as a whole, with outcome data recorded for all new patients who have had the opportunity to engage with an outcome orientated service from the first appointment.

Clear policies should also be developed on how the database of outcomes will be viewed, used, and reported on. We would recommend that outcome data by team level only be reported on to higher management. Supervisors should have access to outcome data by clinician. Decisions will need to be made on who prepares reports, what data from the outcome database to include and how often.

## Supervisor training

Managers will need to support a robust programme of supervisor training in the OO-CAMHS approach. Supervisors and those in leadership positions will have an important role to play in leading the team to develop an Outcome Orientation in their team culture. Supervisors will need extra training and a forum for continuing support and development of the supervisor role should be put in place. This can include a regular supervisors peer group and/or e-mail forum.

# Developing a data base

**This section will cover:**

- Setting up a database on Excel.

- Using the database on © MyOutcomes 2012.

## Using excel

Using excel, a basic table of the patient's ORS/CORS scores can be recorded and graphs generated from this.

| Patient ID | | | | | | | |
|---|---|---|---|---|---|---|---|
| **Session Number** | 1 | 2 | 3 | 4 | 5 | 6 | 7 |
| **Young Person** ORS | 20 | 16 | 20 | 18 | 11 | | |
| **Young Person** SRS | | | | | | | |
| **Parent / Carer** ORS | | | | | | | |
| **Parent / Carer** SRS | | | | | | | |

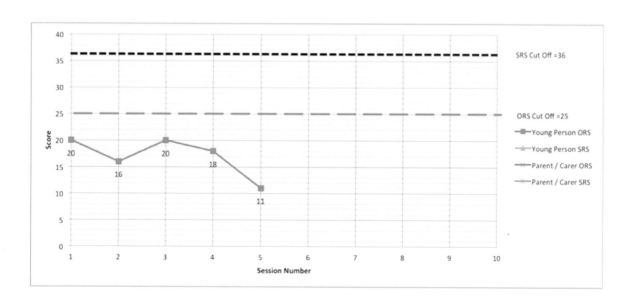

The ORS/CORS scores of all the patients seen by the service can be recorded in a table in excel. The average of final column that records the most recent ORS/CORS score can be compared with the average of the session 1 column to provide an indication of effectiveness of the service.

Spread sheets can be done per service, per presentation, per clinician, and so on.

| | Patient ID | Session 1 | Session 2 | Session 3 | ... | ... | Most recent session |
|---|---|---|---|---|---|---|---|
| 1 | | | | | | | |
| 2 | | | | | | | |
| 3 | | | | | | | |
| 4 | | | | | | | |
| 5 | | | | | | | |

# Using '© MyOutcomes 2012' database

As patient data is entered on '© MyOutcomes 2012' the programme automatically calculates a number of statistics. The breakdown of available data depends on how subdivisions have been structured by the service.

When creating a structure in '© MyOutcomes 2012' 4 levels of organisation are available and aggregated data will be available for each level. The 4 levels are (in descending hierarchy):

*Administrator* (the overall level for the whole service)

*Supervisor* (will usually be teams within the service, but can also be used to represent professional groups, particular specialist interventions (e.g. group work), geographical locations and so on)

*Clinician* (referred to as 'service provider' by '© MyOutcomes 2012')

*Patient group* (referred to as 'client group' by '© MyOutcomes 2012', this level can be divided in a variety of ways depending on the breakdown of data desired by the clinician, for example, by diagnostic grouping, by particular modality of treatment, by geographical location, by age group and so on)

The aggregated data will appear as in the example table below

| Category | Statistic | Active | Inactive |
|---|---|---|---|
| Overall Change | Average Intake ORS | 19.4 | 20.6 |
| | Average Most Recent ORS | 22.9 | 29.4 |
| | Average Raw Change | 4.2 | 10.0 |
| | Uncorrected Effect Size | 0.6 | 1.3 |
| Change vs. Session Targets | Average Change Index | 0.4 | NA |
| | Corrected Effect Size | 0.1 | NA |
| Change vs. Service Targets | Average Change Index | -1.1 | 5.2 |
| | Corrected Effect Size | -0.1 | 0.7 |
| | % of Clients Reaching Service Targets | 47.4 | 76.2 |
| Sessions | Average Sessions | 3.1 | 3.0 |
| Clients | Total Clients | 156 | 148 |

***Active and Inactive*** – Active patients are those that are currently open on the system (i.e. have not been 'deactivated) and represent patients in an on-going episode of care. Inactive patients are those who have completed an episode of care and been 'de-activated' on the system (which means discharged by the service).

***Average Intake ORS*** – The average of the first ORS score of patients.

***Average Most Recent ORS*** – The average ORS score of patients' most recent rating.

***Average Raw Change*** – The average difference in the ORS score between the first and most recent session

***Uncorrected Effect Size*** – Effect size is a measure of the strength of a relationship between two variables. In this case, between the first and most recent ORS scores. For example, an effect size of 0.6 means that the score of the average patient after therapy is 0.6 standard deviations above where they were at the start of therapy. It is convention to rate anything above an effect size of 0.8 as indicating a 'large' change.

***% of Clients Reaching Service Targets*** – refers to the percentage of patients in that group who are above the 50th percentile of the Expected Treatment Response (ETR).

***Average Sessions*** – the average number of sessions (or more accurately the average of the number of times the ORS has been completed and recorded on the system for a given patient) for this patient group.

# Keeping OO on Track

> **This section will cover:**
>
> - Likely problems that could prevent maintenance of a service transformation project.
>
> - Ideas on how to maintain positive gains.

There's an old Dave Allen joke about giving up smoking that goes something like this: *"Giving up smoking is easy. I've done it hundreds of times!"*

Maintaining a change that has happened is an issue well known to family therapists. Groups of people who spend time with each other find themselves slotting into particular roles. In families we often call this the 'family script'. Like a repeated play, each member of the family has their script and whether they like their script or not, because everyone knows what they expect, individuals tend to stick to their script/ role in the family. Therapists then work hard to help families change this script and are often successful in persuading families to do this. However, the real challenge comes after a little bit of time passes. The family script is the default position and members will drift back into this, often without realising they are doing it. How to keep the changes going and made permanent is often the biggest challenge.

So like a family wanting to stop themselves from drifting back to their old script, a successful project will need to keep revisiting their 'scripts' to keep changes on track. Support and attention from management, supervisors, and senior clinicians will be key to this.

## Ideas to keep an OO-CAMHS service transformation project on track:

Data integrity is a critical component of successful service transformation projects. Put in place processes to review data at regular intervals (for example fortnightly or monthly). This will help with picking up clinicians who may not be using the rating scales regularly.

Arrange for regular slots for training or team development as a whole team exercise. We would recommend at least one full day a term. Use the data available to help plan what sort of training or team reflection may be useful (e.g. If as part of your data analysis you have discovered higher drop out rates and worse outcomes for patients with an ethnic minority background, training on culture and mental health, or inviting members of ethnic minority community to discuss their needs may prove useful).

Keep a supervisors peer group going where problems with the transformation project can be addressed

Carry out an audit. An example **Audit Tool** for OO-CAMHS can be found on pages 112 – 115.

Carry out some research. Use the database to carry out some basic research looking at outcomes related to different presentations. Carry out qualitative research to understand clinicians and/or service users impressions of the positives and negatives they associate with the OO-CAMHS model.

# Film – "Introducing OO-CAMHS"

The film 'Introducing OO-CAMHS' provides a brief explanation of the CORE principles and includes film of a young person filling in the ORS and of her mother discussing her results for the SRS. It also includes interviews with and reflections from clinicians using the OO-CAMHS approach. It can be viewed by going to **http:// www.oocamhs.com** clicking on the 'resources' tab and scrolling down to the 'videos' tab.

## Introducing OO-CAMHS

You can also find other useful films there such as the full film of a young person filling in an ORS at her first session and the full film of her mother filling in a SRS at the end of that first session.

There are many other resources on the OO-CAMHS website including articles, hand-outs, and a forum.

# References

Ahm. H., Wampold, B. (2001) Where oh where are the specific ingredients? A meta-analysis of component studies in counselling and psychotherapy. *Journal of Counseling Psychology*, 38, 251-257.

Anderson, T., Lunnen, K.M., Ogles, B.M. (2010) Putting models and techniques in context. In B.L. Duncan, S.D. Miller, B.E. Wampold, M.A. Hubble (Eds.), *The Heart and Soul of Change: Delivering What Works in Therapy (2nd Ed.)*. Washington, DC: American Psychological Association.

Anker, M., Duncan, B., Sparks, J. (2009) Using Client Feedback to Improve Couple Therapy Outcomes: A Randomized Clinical Trial in a Naturalistic Setting. *Journal of Consulting and Clinical Psychology*, 77, 693-704.

Anker, M., Owen, J., Duncan, B., Sparks, J. (2010) The alliance in couple therapy: Partner influence, early change, and alliance patterns in a naturalistic sample. *Journal of Consulting and Clinical Psychology*, 78, 635–645.

Baekeland, F., Lundwall, L. (1975) Dropping out of treatment: A critical review. *Psychological Bulletin*, 82, 738-783.

Barkley, R.A., Fischer, M., Smallish, L., Fletcher, K. (2004) Young adult follow-up of hyperactive children: antisocial activities and drug use. *Journal of Child Psychology and Psychiatry,* 45, 195-211.

Benish, S., Imel, Z.E., Wampold, B.E. (2008) The relative efficacy of bona fide psychotherapies of posttraumatic stress disorder: A meta-analysis of direct comparisons. *Clinical Psychology Review*, 28, 746-758.

Beutler, L.E., Malik, M., Alimohamed, S., Harwood, T. M., Talebi, H., Noble, S. (2004). Therapist variables. In M.J. Lambert (Ed.), *Bergin and Garfield's Handbook of Psychotherapy and Behavior Change (5th Ed.)*. New York: Wiley.

Bickman, L., Guthrie, P.R., Foster, E.M. (1995) *Evaluating Managed Mental Health Services: The Fort Bragg Experiment*. New York: Plenum.

Bickman, L., Lambert, E.W., Andrade, A.R., Penaloza, R. (2000) The Fort Bragg Continuum of Care for Children and Adolescents: Mental Health Outcomes Over Five Years. *Journal of Consulting and Clinical Psychology*, 68, 710-716.

Bickman, L., Summerfelt, W.T., Firth, J., Douglas, S. (1997) The Stark County Evaluation Project: Baseline results of a randomized experiment. In D. Northrup, C. Nixon (Eds.), *Evaluating Mental Health Services: How do Programs for Children "Work" in the Real World?* Newbury Park, CA: Sage Publications.

Biederman, J., Faraone, S., Milberger, S. (1996) A prospective 4-year follow-up study of attention-deficit hyperactivity and related disorders. *Archives of General Psychiatry*, 53, 437-46.

Bringhurst, D.L., Watson, C.W., Miller, S.D., Duncan, B.L. (2006) The reliability and validity of the Outcome Rating Scale: A replication study of a brief clinical measure. *Journal of Brief Therapy*, 5, 23-30.

Campbell, A., Hemsley, S. (2009) Outcome Rating Scale and Session Rating Scale in psychological practice: Clinical utility of ultra-brief measures. *Clinical Psychologist*, 13, 1–9.

Castonguay, L.G., Beutler, L.E. (2005) Common and unique principles of therapeutic change: What do we know and what do we need to know? In L.G. Castonguay, L.E. Beutler (Eds.), *Principles of Therapeutic Change that Work*. New York: Oxford University Press.

Cooper, M. (2008) *Essential Research Findings in Counselling and Psychotherapy: The Facts are Friendly.* London: Sage.

Duncan, B.L. (2012) The Partners for Change Outcome Management System (PCOMS): The Heart and Soul of Change Project. *Canadian Psychology*, 53, 93-104.

Duncan, B., Miller, S., Sparks, J, Claud, D., Reynolds. L., Brown, J., Johnson, L. (2003) The Session Rating Scale: Preliminary psychometric properties of a "working" alliance measure. *Journal of Brief Therapy*, 3, 3-12.

Dunacn, B., Miller, S., Wampold, B., Hubble, M. (2010) *The Heart and Soul of Change (Second Edition)*. Washington DC: American Psychological Association.

Duncan, B., Sparks, J. (2010) *Heroic Clients, Heroic Agencies: Partners for Change (Second Edition)*. Retrieved from: http://www.clientdirectedoutcomeinformed.com/assets/bookstore.aspx

Duncan, B., Sparks, J., Miller, S., Bohanske, R., Claud, D. (2006) Giving youth a voice: A preliminary study of the reliability and validity of a brief outcome measure for children, adolescents, and caretakers. *Journal of Brief Therapy*, 5, 66-82.

Duncan, B. L., Miller, S. D. (2005) Treatment manuals do not improve outcomes. In J.C. Norcross, L.E. Beutler, R.F. Levant (Eds.), *Evidence-Based Practices in Mental Health: Debate and Dialogue on the Fundamental Questions*. Washington, DC: American Psychological Association.

Edlund, M., Wampg, P., Berglund, P., Katz, S., Lin, E., Kessler, R. (2002) Dropping out of mental health treatment: Patterns and predictors among epidemiological survey respondents in the United States and Ontario. *American Journal of Psychiatry*, 159, 845-851.

Evans, R. (2011a) *Comparing the Quality of Psychological Therapy Services on the Basis of Number of Recovered Patients for a Fixed Expenditure*. The Artemis Trust, West Sussex.

Evans, R. (2011b) *Comparing the Quality of Psychological Therapy Services on the Basis of Patient Recovery*. The Artemis Trust, West Sussex.

Fergusson, D.M., Horwood, L.J., & Ridder, E.M. (2007) Conduct and attentional problems in childhood and adolescence and later substance use, abuse and dependence: results of a 25-year longitudinal study. *Drug and Alcohol Dependency*, 88, S14-S26.

Frank, J.D. (1976) Psychotherapy and the sense of mastery. In R.L. Spitzer et al. (Eds), *Evaluation of Psychotherapies*. Baltimore, MD: Johns Hopkins.

Garcia, J.A., Weisz, J.R. (2002) When youth mental health care stops: Therapeutic relationship problems and other reasons for ending youth outpatient treatment. *Journal of Consulting and Clinical Psychology*, 70, 439-443.

Gassman, D. Grawe, K. (2006) General change mechanisms: The relation between problem activation and resource activation in successful and unsuccessful therapeutic interactions. *Clinical Psychology and Psychotherapy*, 13, 1-11.

Gillaspy, J.A., Murphy, J.J. (2011). The use of ultra-brief client feedback tools in SFBT. In C.W. Franklin, T. Trepper, E. McCollum, W. Gingerich (Eds.), *Solution-Focused Brief Therapy*. New York: Oxford University Press.

Hannan, C., Lambert, M. J.,Harmon, C., Nielsen, S. L., Smart, D. W., Shimokawa, K., et al. (2005) A lab test and algorithms for identifying clients at risk for treatment failure. *Journal of Clinical Psychology: In Session*, 61, 155-163.

Hansen, N., Lambert, M., Forman, E. (2002) The psychotherapy dose-effect and its implications for treatment delivery services. *Clinical Psychology: Science and Practice*, 9, 329-343.

Hopper, K., Harrison, G., Janka, A., Sartorius, N. (Eds.) (2007) *Recovery from Schizophrenia: An International Perspective*. Oxford: Oxford University Press.

Howard, K.I., Kopte, S.M., Krause, M.S., Orlinsky, D.E. (1986) The dose-effect relationship in psychotherapy. *American Psychologist*, 41, 159–164.

Howard, K.I, Moras, K., Brill, P.L., Martinovich, Z., Lutz, W. (1996) Evaluation of psychotherapy: Efficacy, effectiveness, and patient progress. *American Psychologist*, 51, 1059-1064.

Hubble, M.A., Duncan, B.L., Miller, S.D., Wampold, B.E. (2010) Introduction. In B.L. Duncan, S.D. Miller, B.E. Wampold, M.A. Hubble (Eds.), *The Heart and Soul of Change: Delivering What Works in Therapy (2nd Ed.)*. Washington, DC: American Psychological Association.

Imel, Z.E., Wampold, B.E. (2008) The common factors of psychotherapy. In S.D. Brown, R.W. Lent (Eds.), *Handbook of Counseling Psychology (4th Ed.)*. New York: Wiley.

Imel, Z.E., Wampold, B.E., Miller, S.D., Fleming, R.R. (2008) Distinctions without a difference: Direct comparisons of psychotherapies for alcohol use disorders. *Journal of Addictive Behaviors*, 22, 533-543.

Jacobson, N.S. (1988) Defining clinically significant change: An introduction. *Behavioral Assessment*, 10, 131-132.

Jacobson, N.S., Folette, W.C., Revenstorf, D. (1984) Psychotherapy outcome research: Methods for reporting variability and evaluating clinical significance. *Behavior Therapy*, 15, 336-352.

Jacobson, N.S., Truax, P. (1991) Clinical significance: A statistical approach to defining meaningful change in psychotherapy research. *Journal of Consulting and Clinical Psychology*, 59, 12-19.

Jacobson, N.S., Dobson, K.S., Truax, P.A., Addis, M., Koerner, K. et al. (1996) A component analysis of cognitive-behavioural treatment for depression. *Journal of Consulting and Clinical Psychology*, 64, 295-304.

Karver, M., Handelsman, J., Fields, S., Bickman, L. (2005) A theoretical model of common process factors in youth and family therapy. *Mental Health Services Research*, 7, 35-51.

Kazdin, A.E. (2004) Psychotherapy for children and adolescents. In M.J. Lambert (Ed.), *Bergin and Garfield's Handbook of Psychotherapy and Behavior Change, 5th Edition*. New York: Wiley.

Kazdin, A.E. (1996) Dropping out of child psychotherapy: Issues for research and implications for practice. *Child Clinical Psychology*, 1, 133-156.

Kirsch, I. (2009) *The Emperor's New Drugs: Exploding the Antidepressant Myth*. London: The Bodley Head.

Kirsch, I., Deacon, B.J., Huedo-Medina, T.B., Scoboria, A., Moore, T.J., Johnson, B.T. (2008) Initial severity and antidepressant benefits: a meta-analysis of data submitted to the Food and Drug Administration. *Public Library of Science: Medicine*, 5, e45.

Lambert, M. (2004) *Bergin and Garfield's Handbook of Psychotherapy and Behavior Change, Fifth Edition*. New York: John Wiley.

Lambert, M. (2010) Yes, it is time for clinicians to routinely monitor treatment outcome. In B.L. Duncan, S.D. Miller, B.E. Wampold, M.A Hubble (Eds.), *The Heart and Soul of Change (Second Edition)*. Washington, DC: American Psychological Association.

Lambert, M.J., Shimokawa, K. (2011) Collecting client feedback. In J.C. Norcross (Ed.), *Psychotherapy Relationships that Work (Second Edition)*. New York: Oxford University Press.

Lambert, M.J., Hill, C.E. (1994) Assessing psychotherapy outcomes and processes. In A.E. Bergin, S.L. Garfield (Eds.), *Handbook of Psychotherapy and Behavior Change (4th Ed)*. New York: Wiley.

Lee, S.S., Hinshaw, S.P. (2004) Severity of adolescent delinquency among boys with and without attention deficit hyperactivity disorder: predictions from early antisocial behavior and peer status. *Journal of Clinical Child and Adolescent Psychology*, 33, 705-16.

Liberman, B. (1978) The maintenance and persistence of change.  In J.D. Frank et al. (Eds), *Effective Ingredients of Effective Psychotherapy*. New York: Brunner Mazel.

Longmore, R.J., Worrell, M. (2007) Do we need to challenge thoughts in cognitive behaviour therapy? *Clinical Psychology Review*, 27, 173-87.

March, J.S., and the TADS team (2007) The Treatment for Adolescents With Depression Study (TADS): long-term effectiveness and safety outcomes. *Archives of General Psychiatry*, 64, 1132–1143.

Miller, S.D., Duncan, B.L., Brown, J., Sorrell, R., Chalk, M.B. (2006) Using formal client feedback to improve retention and outcomes. *Journal of Brief Therapy*, 5, 5-22.

Miller, S., Duncan, B., Brown, J., Sparks, J., Claud, D. (2003) The Outcome Rating Scale: A preliminary study of reliability, validity, and feasibility of a brief visual analogue measure. *Journal of Brief Therapy*, 2, 91-100.

Miller, S., Wampold, B., Varhely, K. (2008) Direct comparisons of treatment modalities for youth disorders: a meta-analysis. *Psychotherapy Research*, 18, 5-14.

Miller, S.D., Duncan, B.L. (2000) *The Heroic Client*. San Francisco: Jossey-Bass.

Miller, S.L., Duncan, B.L, Sorrell, R., Brown, G.S. (2005) The partners for change outcome management system. *Journal of Clinical Psychology*, 61, 199-208.

Miller, S.D., Duncan, B.L., Hubble, M.A. (2007) Supershrinks. *Psychotherapy Networker*, 31(6), 26-35.

Miller, S.D., Duncan, B.L., Sorrell, R., Brown, G.S. (2004) The Partners for Change Outcome Management System. *Journal of Clinical Psychology*, 6, 199-208.

Moncrieff, J. (2009) *The Myth of the Chemical Cure*. Basingstoke: Palgrave MacMillan.

MTA Co-operative Group (1999) A 14 month randomized clinical trial of treatment strategies for attention deficit/hyperactivity disorder. *Archives of General Psychiatry*, 56, 1073–1086.

Norcross, J.C., Goldfried, M.R. (1992). *Handbook of Psychotherapy Integration*. New York: Basic Books.

Orlinsky, D.E., Rønnestad, M.H., Willutzki, U. (2004) Fifty years of psychotherapy process-outcome research: Continuity and change. In M.J. Lambert (Ed.), *Bergin and Garfield's Handbook of Psychotherapy and Behavior Change (5th Ed.)*. New York: Wiley.

Pekarik, G. (1992) Post-treatment adjustment of clients who drop out early vs late in Treatment. *Journal of Clinical Psychology*, 48, 379-387.

Reese, R., Norsworthy, L., Rowlands, S. (2009) Does a continuous feedback model improve psychotherapy outcomes? *Psychotherapy: Theory, Research, Practice, Training*, 46, 418-431.

Reese, R., Toland, M., Slone, N., Norsworthy, L. (2010) Effect of client feedback on couple psychotherapy outcomes. *Psychotherapy*, 47, 616-630.

Nyman, S.J., Nafziger, M.A., Smith, T.B. (2010) Client outcomes across counselor training level within a multi-tiered supervision model. *Journal of Counseling and Development*, 88, 204-209.

Rosenzweig, S. (1936) Some implicit common factors in diverse methods of psychotherapy. *American Journal of Orthopsychiatry*, 6, 412–415.

Sapyta, J., Reimer, M., Bickman, L. (2005) Feedback to clinicians: theory, research and practice. *Journal of Clinical Psychology*, 61, 145-153.

Shadish, W.R, Baldwin, S.S. (2002). Meta-analysis of MFT interventions. In D.H. Sprenkle (Ed.), *Effectiveness Research in Marital and Family Therapy*. Alexandria, VA: American Association for Marriage and Family Therapy.

Smith, M.L., Glass, G.V., Miller, T.I. (1980). *The Benefits of Psychotherapy*. Baltimore: John Hopkins University Press.

Sparks, J., Duncan, B., Miller, S. (2008). Common factors in psychotherapy: Common means to uncommon outcomes. In J. Lebow (Ed.) *21st Century Psychotherapies*. New York: Wiley.

Spielmans, G.I., Pasek, L.F., McFall, J.P. (2007) What are the active ingredients in cognitive and behavioral psychotherapy for anxious and depressed children? A meta-analytic review. *Clinical Psychology Review*, 27, 642-654

Stiles, W.B., Barkham, M., Mellor-Car, J. (2008) Effectiveness of cognitive-behavioural, person-centred, and psychodynamic therapies in UK primary-care routine practice: replication in a larger sample. *Psychological Medicine*, 38, 677-688.

Timimi, S. (2008) Child psychiatry and its relationship to the pharmaceutical industry Theoretical and practical issues. *Advances in Psychiatric Treatment*, 14, 3-9.

Timimi, S. (2009) *A straight Talking Introduction to Children's Mental Health Problems*. Ross-on-Wye: PCCS Books.

Treatment for Adolescents with Depression Study Team. (2004) Fluoxetine, cognitive–behavioral therapy, and their combination for adolescents with depression: Treatment for Adolescents With Depression Study (TADS) Randomized Controlled Trial. *Journal of the American Medical Association*, 292, 807–820.

Wampold, B.E. (2001) *The Great Psychotherapy Debate: Models, Methods, and Findings*. Mahwah, NJ: Erlbaum.

Walfish, S., McAllister, B., Lambert, M.J. (2010, unpublished) Are all therapists from Lake Wobegon? An investigation of self assessment bias in health providers.

Wampold, B.E. (2007) Psychotherapy: The humanistic (and effective) treatment. American Psychologist, 62, 857-873.

Wampold, B., Brown, J. (2006) Estimating variability in outcomes attributable to therapists: A naturalistic study of outcomes in managed care. *Journal of Consulting and Clinical Psychology*, 73, 914-923.

Wampold, B.E., Mondin, G.W., Moody, M., Stich, F., Benson, K., Ahn, H. (1997) A meta-analysis of outcome studies comparing bona fi de psychotherapies: Empirically, "All Must Have Prizes." *Psychological Bulletin*, 122, 203-215.

Wampold, B.E., Minami, T., Baskin, T.W., Tierney, S.C. (2002) A meta-re(analysis) of the effects of cognitive therapy versus "other therapies" for depression. *Journal of Affective Disorders*, 68, 159-165.

Webb, C.A., DeRubeis, R.J., Barber, J.P. (2010) Therapist adherence/competence and treatment outcome: A meta-analytic review. *Journal of Consulting and Clinical Psychology*, 78, 200-211.

Weiss, B., Catron, T., Harris, V., (1999) The effectiveness of traditional child psychotherapy. *Journal of Consulting and Clinical Psychology*, 67, 82–94.

Weiss, B., Catron, T., Harris, V. (2000) A two-year follow-up of the effectiveness of traditional child psychotherapy. *Journal of Consulting and Clinical Psychology*, 68, 1094–1101.

Weisz, J.R., Donenberg, G.R., Weiss, B. (1995) Bridging the gap between laboratory and clinic in child and adolescent psychotherapy: efficacy and effectiveness in studies of child and adolescent psychotherapy. *Journal of Consulting and Clinical Psychology*, 63, 688–701.

Weisz, J.R., McCarty, C.A., Valeri, S.M. (2006) Effects of psychotherapy for depression in children and adolescents: A meta-analysis. *Psychological Bulletin*, 132, 132-149.

Wierzbicki, M., Pekarik,G. (1993) A meta-analysis of psychotherapy dropout. *Professional Psychology: Research and Practice*, 24, 190-195.

# Websites

**The OO-CAMHS Website** – The OO-CAMHS website includes many useful resources such as articles, hand-outs, film, links to other useful websites and so on. It also includes details on the trainings offered by the OO-CAMHS team. http://www.oocamhs.com

**The Heart and Soul of Change Project** - The Heart and Soul of Change Project (HSCP) is a practice-driven, training and research initiative that focuses on what works in therapy, and more importantly, how to deliver it on the front lines via patient based outcome feedback, or what is called the 'Partners for Change Outcome Management Systems' (PCOMS). http://heartandsoulofchange.com

**Outcome Orientated Approaches to Mental Health Services (OO-AMHS) e-Learning Modules** – E-learning modules for individuals and/or mental health service teams in the application of an Outcome Orientated approach to delivery of mental health services. http://www.innovationforlearning.com/LPFT

**My Outcomes** – My Outcomes is a patient-driven outcome management system that solicits direct consumer feedback, encourages individualized service delivery, and enables ongoing monitoring of service effectiveness for providers, agencies, provider networks and managed care organizations in the public and private sectors. **https://www.myoutcomes.com/**

**Regional Innovation Award 2010/2011** - NHS East Midlands provides strategic leadership to the NHS organisations with the aim of creating a stronger health system that is evidence-based, patient-centred, safe, high quality and championed by clinicians.

**http://www.tin.nhs.uk/innovation-nhs-east-midlands/innovation-in-practice/ regional-innovation-fund-projects-2010-11/outcome-orientated-child/**

# Appendix (Rating Scales, Audit, and KPIs)

**Please note that the copies of rating scales are specimen copies only and not suitable for use.** To download your free copies of the rating scales for personal use only please go to **www.heartandsoulofchange.com** or **www.oocamhs.com** and following the links to **ORS/SRS** download.

1.   Specimen copy of ORS

2.   Specimen copy of graph for plotting ORS

3.   Specimen copy of SRS

4.   Specimen copy of CORS

5.   Specimen copy of CSRS

6.   Specimen copy of GSRS

7.   Example of OO-CAMHS Audit template

8.   Example table of Key Performance Indicators (KPIs)

# Outcome Rating Scale (ORS)

Looking back over the last week, including today, help us understand how you have been feeling by rating how well you have been doing in the following areas of your life, where marks to the left represent low levels and marks to the right indicate high levels. *If you are filling out this form for another person, please fill out according to how you think he or she is doing.*

**ATTENTION CLINICIAN**: TO INSURE SCORING ACCURACY PRINT OUT THE MEASURE TO INSURE THE ITEM LINES ARE 10 CM IN LENGTH.  ALTER THE FORM UNTIL THE LINES PRINT THE CORRECT LENGTH.  THEN ERASE THIS MESSAGE.

## Individually

(Personal well-being)

|------------------------------------------------------------------------------------|

## Interpersonally

(Family, close relationships)

|------------------------------------------------------------------------------------|

## Socially

(Work, school, friendships)

|------------------------------------------------------------------------------------|

## Overall

(General sense of well-being)

|------------------------------------------------------------------------------------|

The Heart and Soul of Change Project

www.heartandsoulofchange.com

© 2000, Scott D. Miller and Barry L. Duncan

# Graph for plotting scores

| Session Number | 1 | 2 | 3 | 4 | 5 | 6 | 7 | 8 | 9 | 10 |
|---|---|---|---|---|---|---|---|---|---|---|
| 40 | | | | | | | | | | |
| 35 | | | | | | | | | | |
| 30 | | | | | | | | | | |
| 25 | | | | | | | | | | |
| 20 | ▬ | ▬ | ▬ | ▬ | ▬ | ▬ | ▬ | ▬ | ▬ | ▬ |
| 15 | | | | | | | | | | |
| 10 | | | | | | | | | | |
| 5 | | | | | | | | | | |
| 0 | | | | | | | | | | |

↑
SRS Cutoff
↓
Discuss
↑
ORS CUTOFF

# Session Rating Scale (SRS V.3.0)

Please rate today's session by placing a mark on the line nearest to the description that best fits your experience.

## Relationship

I did not feel heard, understood, and respected.    |-------------------------------------------------------------|    I felt heard, understood, and respected.

## Goals and Topics

We did *not* work on or talk about what I wanted to work on and talk about.    |-------------------------------------------------------------|    We worked on and talked about what I wanted to work on and talk about.

## Approach or Method

The therapist's approach is not a good fit for me.    |-------------------------------------------------------------|    The therapist's approach is a good fit for me.

## Overall

There was something missing in the session today.    |-------------------------------------------------------------|    Overall, today's session was right for me.

The Heart and Soul of Change Project

www.heartandsoulofchange.com

© 2002, Scott D. Miller, Barry L. Duncan, & Lynn Johnson

# Child Outcome Rating Scale (CORS)

How are you doing? How are things going in your life? Please make a mark on the scale to let us know. The closer to the smiley face, the better things are. The closer to the frowny face, things are not so good. *If you are a caretaker filling out this form, please fill out according to how you think the child is doing.*

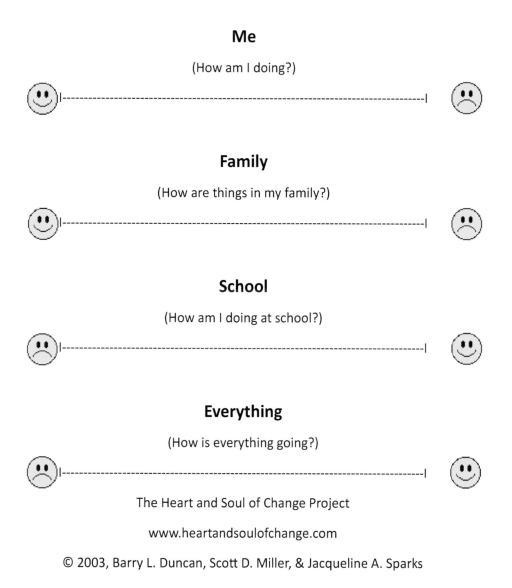

**Me**

(How am I doing?)

**Family**

(How are things in my family?)

**School**

(How am I doing at school?)

**Everything**

(How is everything going?)

The Heart and Soul of Change Project

www.heartandsoulofchange.com

© 2003, Barry L. Duncan, Scott D. Miller, & Jacqueline A. Sparks

# Child Session Rating Scale (CSRS)

_____

How was our time together today? Please put a mark on the lines below to let us know how you feel.

_____

## Listening

You did not always
listen to me.  You listened to me

## How Important

What we did and talked
about was not really
that important to me.  What we did and
talked about were
important to me.

## What We Did

I did not like what
we did today.  I liked what we
did today.

## Overall

I wish we could do
something different.  I hope we do the
same kind of things
next time.

The Heart and Soul of Change Project

www.heartandsoulofchange.com

© 2003, Barry L. Duncan, Scott D. Miller, Jacqueline A. Sparks

# Group Session Rating Scale (GSRS)

Please rate today's group by placing a mark on the line nearest to the description that best fits your experience.

## Relationship

I did not feel understood, respected, and/or accepted by the leader and/or the group.

|----------------------------------------------------------------------|

I felt understood, respected, and accepted by the leader and the group.

## Goals and Topics

We did *not* work on or talk about what I wanted to work on and talk about.

|----------------------------------------------------------------------|

We worked on and talked about what I wanted to work on and talk about.

## Approach or Method

The leader and/or the group's approach are/is not a good fit for me.

|----------------------------------------------------------------------|

The leader and the group's approach are a good fit for me.

## Overall

There was something missing in group today—I did not feel like a part of the group.

|----------------------------------------------------------------------|

Overall, today's group was right for me—I felt like a part of the group.

The Heart and Soul of Change Project

www.heartandsoulofchange.com

© 2007, Barry L. Duncan and Scott D. Miller

# Lincolnshire Partnership **NHS**

NHS Trust

## *Audit of Orientated Outcome procedures in CAMHS*

*Complete one form for each case.*

| Location: | Sex: M / F | Age: | Ethnicity: | Ref No: |
|---|---|---|---|---|
| | | | | |

| Standard No. | Criterion | Yes | No | NA/ Exceptions |
|---|---|---|---|---|
| 1 | Is there evidence that another agency (e.g. social services) is involved in addressing the problems the patient is referred for? <br><br> • If YES, have multi-agency discussions/consultations taken place? | ☐ <br><br><br><br> ☐ | ☐ <br><br><br><br> ☐ | |
| | (Data source: patient record) | | | |
| 2 | Is there evidence the Outcome Rating Scale (ORS) has been administered at each appointment and the score recorded for either or both: <br><br> a.  The young person? ☐ <br> b.  The parent/carer? ☐ <br><br><br> •  If NO – is the reason for not using the ORS documented in the patient notes? <br><br> Has a graph been used to plot the ORS scores so that patient progress can be observed? | <br><br><br><br><br><br><br><br> ☐ <br><br> ☐ | <br><br><br><br><br><br><br><br> ☐ <br><br> ☐ | |
| | (Data source: patient record/online database) | | | |

| Standard No. | Criterion | Yes | No | NA/ Exceptions |
|---|---|---|---|---|
| 3 | Is there evidence that the Session Rating Scale (SRS) is being administered each appointment with either or both:<br><br>a. The young person? ☐<br>b. The parent/carer? ☐<br><br>• If NO – is the reason for not using the SRS documented in the patient notes?<br><br>Is there evidence of SRS scores of 36 or below?<br>• If YES, is there a record that this has been discussed with the person(s) who did the rating? | ☐<br>☐<br>☐ | ☐<br>☐<br>☐ | |
| | (Data source: patient record/online database) | | | |
| 4 | Is there evidence that improvement/progress has been made after the first five sessions?<br><br>• If NO progress made, is there evidence in the notes of discussions about a possible change of approach? | ☐<br><br>☐ | ☐<br><br>☐ | |
| | (Data source: patient record/online database) | | | |

# Lincolnshire Partnership NHS

NHS Trust

## *Clinician Audit of Outcome Orientated Child and Adolescent Mental Health Services (OO-CAMHS)*

### *One form to be completed by each clinician in the CAMHS team*

| Location: | Job Title: |
|---|---|
| | |

| No. | Criterion | Yes | No | NA/ Exceptions |
|---|---|---|---|---|
| 1 | Is it your experience that cases that are not improving after 5 or more sessions are being discussed in team meetings and/or supervision? | ☐ | ☐ | |
| 2 | Do you feel you are getting enough of the right sort of supervision for cases that are not improving? | ☐ | ☐ | |
| 3 | Do you feel valued as an important member of the Multi Disciplinary Team? | ☐ | ☐ | |

| No. | Criterion | Yes | No | NA/ Exceptions |
|-----|-----------|-----|-----|----------------|
| 4 | If you have any comments/observations you wish to make about your experience of the MDT please do so in the space provided below. **Comments:** | | | |

Many thanks for your participation in this audit – your views will play an important part in future service development.

# Example Key Performance Indicators

## OO-CAMHS - Key Performance Indicators (KPI's)

| Area | KPI | Description | Data Source | Actual Number | Out of a total number of | Percentage (%) |
|------|-----|-------------|-------------|---------------|--------------------------|----------------|
| **Service Activity** | Number and % of patients who have completed treatment | This is a count of all those who have completed treatment within the reporting period. The % is the number completed treatment divided by the total closed episodes of treatment (completed + dropped out of treatment + referred to another service).<br><br>Include only those people who have had at least two treatment sessions.<br><br>N.B. This excludes people who had an initial assessment but did not enter treatment. Patients who have a single combined assessment/therapeutic session are unable to provide end of care pathway clinical outcome data. | | | | |
| | Number and % of patients who dropped out of treatment prior to discharge | This is the total number of all those who dropped out of treatment prior to the episode of treatment being completed, within the reporting period. The % is the number who dropped out of treatment divided by the total closed episodes of treatment (completed + dropped out of treatment + referred to another service). | | | | |

| | | | | | | |
|---|---|---|---|---|---|---|
| | Number and % of patients who did not attend (DNA) | This is the total number of non-attendances without informing the service within the reporting period. The % is the number of DNA sessions divided by the total number of sessions offered in the reporting period.<br><br>N.B. It is recommended that you exclude non-attendance rates for first appointments, so that this measure is more reflective of engagement with the service once at least one meeting has taken place. | | | | |
| | Number and % of patients who cancelled appointments | This is the total number of cancelled sessions within the reporting period. The % is the number of cancelled sessions divided by the total number of sessions offered in the reporting period.<br><br>N.B. It is recommended that you exclude cancellation rates for first appointments, so that this measure is more reflective of engagement with the service once at least one meeting has taken place. | | | | |
| | Number and % with the service for over 1 year | This is the total number of those who have been receiving a service for over 12 months. The % is the number open to the service for more than 12 months divided by the total number of open cases at the end of the reporting period. | | | | |
| | Number and % with the service for over 2 years | This is the total number of those who have been receiving a service for over 24 months. The % is the number open to the service for more than 24 months divided by the total number of open cases at the end of the reporting period. | | | | |
| | Number and % referred to another service | This is the total number of those who have been referred to another service in the reporting period. The % is the number referred to another service divided by the total number of open cases in the reporting period. | | | | |

| | | | | | | |
|---|---|---|---|---|---|---|
| | Number and % referred to Specialist Services | This is the total number of those who have been referred to specialist services in the reporting period.  The % is the number referred to specialist services divided by the total number of open cases in the reporting period. | | | | |
| | Number and % referred to inpatient services | This is the total number of those who have been referred to inpatient services in the reporting period. The % is the number referred to inpatient services divided by the total number of open cases in the reporting period. | | | | |
| | Number of complaints | Number of complaints received about the service during the reporting period. | | | | |
| **Moving to Recovery** | Average Overall Change (on the ORS) for open cases | The average difference between the intake (first session) ORS score and the most recent ORS score for cases still open at the end of the reporting period, to include young person and/or parent/carer scores.<br><br>Analysis is based on patients still in treatment who may not have reached their full change potential. A score of 0 or below indicates no progress; a score of 5 or greater indicates a reliable significant clinical change. | | | | |
| | Average Overall Change (on the ORS) for discharged cases | The average difference between the intake ORS score and most recent ORS score for cases discharged during the reporting period, to include young person and/or parent/carer scores.<br><br>Analysis is based on patients who have completed treatment and been discharged. A score of 0 or below indicates no progress; a score of 5 or greater indicates a reliable significant clinical change. | | | | |

| | | | | | | |
|---|---|---|---|---|---|---|
| | Number and % with an improvement of 5 points or more on the ORS by discharge | The total number of patients whose ORS score has increased by 5 points or more by discharge during the reporting period to include young person and/or parent/carer scores. The % is obtained by dividing this number by the total number of patients discharged in the reporting period. | | | | |
| | Number and % of Patients above clinical cut off by discharge | The number of patients who are rating above the clinical cut off on the ORS by discharge during the reporting period to include young person and/or parent/carer scores. The % is obtained by dividing this number by the total number of patients discharged in the reporting period. | | | | |
| **Building an OO-CAMHS Service** | Number and % of staff trained in OO-CAMHS at the end of the reporting period. | The number of staff trained in OO-CAMHS. The percentage is this number divided by the total number of clinical staff in the service. | | | | |
| | Number and % of supervisors and managers trained at the end of the reporting period | The number of supervisors and managers trained in OO-CAMHS supervision and management. The percentage is this number divided by the total number of supervisors/managers in the service. | | | | |
| | Number and % of outcome ratings completed at desired frequency. | Number of patients with complete outcome data recorded. The % is this number divided by the total number of patients seen in the reporting period. | | | | |
| | Number and % of alliance ratings completed at desired frequency. | Number of patients with complete alliance data recorded. The % is this number divided by the total number of patients seen in the reporting period. | | | | |
| | Number and % of graphic display of outcomes available. | Number of patients where records of outcomes have been put onto a graph that can be seen by patients. The % is this number divided by the total number of patients seen in the reporting period. | | | | |

| | | | | | | |
|---|---|---|---|---|---|---|
| | Number and % where discussion has taken place and recorded if there is no progress on ORS after 5 sessions | Number of patients where discussions have taken place (with patient and/or MDT) and are recoded in notes, when there is no progress by session 5. The % is this number divided by the total number of patients who have not made progress on the ORS by session 5 in the reporting period. | | | | |
| | Number and % of consultations that have taken place where there is multi-agency involvement | Number of patients where consultations/discussions with other professional and/or agencies that have taken place when there is more than one agency or clinician working with the patient in the reporting period. The % is this number divided by the total number of cases open simultaneously to more than one clinician or agency. | | | | |
| | Number and % of clinicians attending team meetings for clinical discussion regularly (such as weekly) | Number of clinicians attending clinical case discussion meetings at the prescribed frequency. The % is this number divided by the total number of clinicians. | | | | |

# Our contact details

**Sami Timimi**

Consultant child and Adolescent Psychiatrist
Lincolnshire Partnership Foundation NHS Trust
Child and Adolescent Mental Health Services,
Horizon Centre
Homer House
Sibthorpe Street
Lincoln
Lincolnshire
LN5 7SL

Tel: 01522 535189
e-mail: **stimimi@talk21.com**

**Dianne Tetley**

Assistant Director Research and Effectiveness
Lincolnshire Partnership NHS Foundation Trust
Research and Effectiveness Department
Room 2203, Bridge House
University of Lincoln
Brayford Pool
Lincoln
LN6 7TS

Tel: Lincoln - 01522 837032 (Wednesday and Thursday)
      Sleaford - 01529 222221 (Monday, Tuesday and Friday)
e-mail: **Dianne.Tetley@lpft.nhs.uk**

**Wayne Burgoine**

Senior Clinical Psychologist,
Latrobe Regional Hospital GCAMHS Team,
Community Mental Health Services,
McKean Street,
Bairnsdale, VIC 3875.
Australia

e-mail: **wayneburgoine@hotmail.com**

"OO-CAMHS could very well begin to change the face of mental health care in the UK"

**Barry Duncan**

OO-CAMHS is a whole service model that incorporates existing evidence on how to improve outcomes, reduce non-attendance and dropout rates and save money through improved therapeutic efficiency. This service transformation toolkit covers every aspect of improving the mental health of children and young people that any clinician and team needs to know about. From the evidence base to the clinical encounter to management and supervision, this toolkit will enable your service to experience the benefits of a radical revolution in young peoples' mental healthcare.

Lightning Source UK Ltd.
Milton Keynes UK
UKRC02n0159061216
289282UK00006B/43

9 781477 219409